DATE DUE			

Lazarillo de Tormes

Twayne's World Authors Series
Spanish Literature

Janet Pérez, Editor
Texas Tech University

Donald W. Bleznick, Editor
University of Cincinnati

TWAS 714

Lazarillo de Tormes

By Robert L. Fiore

Michigan State University

Twayne Publishers • Boston

Lazarillo de Tormes

Robert L. Fiore

Copyright © 1984 by G. K. Hall & Company
All Rights Reserved
Published by Twayne Publishers
A Division of G. K. Hall & Company
70 Lincoln Street
Boston, Massachusetts 02111

Book Production by Marne B. Sultz
Book Design by Barbara Anderson

Printed on permanent/durable acid-free
paper and bound in the United States of
America.

Library of Congress Cataloging in Publication Data

Fiore, Robert L.
  Lazarillo de Tormes.

  (Twayne's world authors series; TWAS 714
Spanish literature)
  Bibliography: p. 119
  Includes index.
  1. Lazarillo de Tormes. I. Title II. Series:
Twayne's world authors series; TWAS 714. III. Series:
Twayne's world authors series. Spanish literature.
PQ6409.F56   1984   863'.3   83–22633
ISBN 0–8057–6561–1

In memory of Charles D. Blend,
a true humanist and friend

But Fortune had a smile left
for me when in utter calamity;
perhaps she merely wanted to
preserve me for further mishaps. . .

Apuleius

Contents

About the Author

Robert L. Fiore is assistant dean of the College of Arts and Letters at Michigan State University and professor in the Department of Romance and Classical Languages where he has taught Spanish and Italian since 1967. Prior to that he taught at the University of North Carolina at Greensboro. Born in New York, he studied in the United States and Spain, and received his B.A. from Iona College, his M.A. from Middlebury College, and his Ph.D. in Romance Languages from the University of North Carolina at Chapel Hill. He has published *Drama and Ethos: A Study of Natural-Law Ethics in Spanish Golden Age Theater* (1975), a book that was well received by the critics. He has also published numerous articles on Golden Age literature including important studies on Lope, Tirso, Calderón, Alarcón, the *Lazarillo* and the Picaresque.

Preface

The amazing literary career of *Lazarillo de Tormes* begins in 1554, in Antwerp, Burgos, and Alcalá. The book, which was an influential progenitor of the novel, serves as the model for the picaresque genre. It is a work that drew attention from the start, and its popularity has not waned in the years since it first appeared; indeed, it is considered by most critics to be second in popularity and acclaim only to *Don Quixote* in Spanish literature. The many editions, translations, and studies of the work attest to this. As the most important and influential novel of the picaresque genre, *Lazarillo de Tormes* has had a marked influence on writers of Spain, Great Britain, Germany, France, Italy, and Latin America.

Innumerable scholarly and critical studies have been written on the novel's innovative technique and style, subjects which to this day have not been exhausted. Scholars have also been intrigued by the mystery that surrounds its anonymity and the *princeps* edition.

The present study proposes to give the general reader an introduction to and an understanding and appreciation of the novelistic genius of *Lazarillo de Tormes*. In the limited space available I have dealt with the most important problems and themes associated with the work; the picaresque genre; the problems concerning editions; continuations and early translations; the anonymous author; the analysis of the novel itself; and the narrative technique and style. In my study I refer to the young protagonist of the first four chapters as Lazarillo and to the adult character and narrator as Lázaro.

Almost all of the quotations from the novel are in English and are my renditions of the original Spanish. I have included some Spanish when I deemed it necessary to understand the figurative language, style, puns, and the like. The Spanish is taken from the readily available and well-annotated edition of Joseph V. Ricapito.

I wish to record my gratitude to my colleagues and friends who have contributed in various ways to the completion of this study. I am especially indebted to Frieda Brown and George Mansour of Michigan State University for their many valuable suggestions, and to Malcolm Compitello and Dennis Seniff for their thoughtful reading of the typescript.

My special thanks to Michigan State University for the generous grant of sabbatical leave that enabled me to finish the book, to Henry Koch and the library staff for their help, and to Cathy Sparks for the finished typescript. Finally I thank my children, David and Gabriella, for just being the way they are.

Robert L. Fiore

Michigan State University

Chronology

1510   Expedition of García of Toledo to Gelves.

1516   Charles V (as king of Spain, Charles I) begins his reign.

1519   Charles is elected Holy Roman Emperor.

1525   Battle of Pavia. Charles V defeats and imprisons Francis I. Parliament held in Toledo.

1538–1539   Second Parliament held in Toledo.

1554   *La vida de Lazarillo de Tormes y de sus fortunas y adversidades* appears in three distinct editions in Burgos, Alcalá de Henares, and Antwerp.

1555   The anonymous *Segunda parte de la vida de Lazarillo de Tormes,* the first continuation of the original work, is published in Antwerp. It is later reprinted with the first part, in Milan (1587, 1615) and in Spain for the first time in 1844.

1556   Charles V abdicates; Philip II succeeds to the throne.

1559   *Lazarillo de Tormes* banned by the Grand Inquisitor's *Cathalogus librorum qui prohibentur* which appears in Valladolid.

1573   Censored edition of *Lazarillo de Tormes* is printed in Madrid by the royal chronicler and cosmographer Juan López de Velasco.

1573–1595   *Lazarillo de Tormes* is reprinted five times in Tarragona (1586), in Milan (1587), in Antwerp (1595), and in Bergamo (1597).

1560   First French translation appears in Lyon. It is reprinted in Paris (1561). Bilingual edition is published in 1660.

1568   First English translation by David Rowland. Others follow (1586, 1596, 1624, 1631).

1598   Philip II dies; he is succeeded by Philip III who reigns until 1621.

1599 Mateo Alemán's *Guzmán de Alfarache* and López de Ubeda's *La Pícara Justina*.

1605 Cervantes's *Don Quixote*, part 1.

1608 First Italian translation of *Lazarillo de Tormes* is published in Venice. Others later appear in Venice (1622, 1635, 1636).

1613 Cervantes's *Novelas ejemplares*.

1615 *Don Quixote*, part 2. First published German translation of *Lazarillo de Tormes* appears in Augsburg (1617).

1618 Vicente Espinel's *La vida del escudero Marcos de Obregón*.

1620 Juan de Luna's *Segunda parte de Lazarillo de Tormes* is published in Paris. Juan Cortés de Tolosa's *Lazarillo de Manzanares* is published in Madrid.

1623 Gaspar Ens publishes a Latin translation of the *Lazarillo* based on the Augsburg translation of 1617.

1626 Francisco Quevedo's *La vida del buscón*.

1646 *La vida y hechos de Estebanillo González, hombre de buen humor.*

Chapter One
The Picaresque Genre

The term picaresque has drawn the attention of many critics from various countries and has suffered the same fate as other literary terms such as romanticism, realism, naturalism, irony, and satire. It has produced a considerable amount of confusion as critics attempted to redefine it to make it usable or to suit their own purposes. This chapter, which is not exhaustive, deals with the most significant work on the picaresque and is intended to give the reader an understanding of the genre and how it relates to *Lazarillo de Tormes*. The pioneer work on picaresque fiction, Frank Wadleigh Chandler's *Romances of Roguery,* published in 1899, offers a workable definition of the term:

The picaresque novel of the Spaniards presents a rogue relating his adventures. He is born of poor and dishonest parents, who are not often troubled with gracing their union by a ceremony, nor particularly pleased at his advent. He comes up by hook or crook as he may. Either he enters the world with an innate love of the goods of others, or he is innocent and learns by hard raps that he must take care of himself or go to the wall. In either case the result is much the same; in order to live he must serve somebody, and the gains of service he finds himself obliged to augment with the gains of roguery. So he flits from one master to another, all of whom he outwits in his career, and describes to satirize in his narrative. Finally, having run through a variety of strange vicissitudes, measuring by his rule of roguery the vanity of human estates, he brings his story to a close.[1]

Chandler's description of the picaresque focuses on the *pícaro* as rogue narrator and is general in scope, but does distinguish the picaresque novel from other literature of roguery.

In recent years, however, it has become increasingly difficult for critics to establish a clear definition of the term picaresque. In part, the problem stems from an international cultural lag and a lack of familiarity with primary and secondary sources of Spanish picaresque fiction. Consequently, many non-Hispanists tend to use the term in too broad a sense, and frequently include as picaresque fic-

1

tion any literature whose hero is on a journey or has several masters.
The hero may range from a criminal type to a gentleman or lady
who, because of circumstances, spends time with the lower classes.
On the other hand, some Hispanists have been too restrictive, considering the picaresque to be a genre limited exclusively to Golden
Age Spain. An example of the confusion which results from too
broad an interpretation is the observation that Kay Seymour House
makes in her book, *Cooper's Americans*. She maintains that
Hawkeye, the protagonist of *The Last of the Mohicans*, is somewhere
between the *picaro* of the eighteenth-century narrative and the
possessed irrational hero of Gothic romance. She even includes *Don
Quixote* in her sweeping definition of the picaresque: "The great
prototype who is both *picaro* and possessed is of course Don Quixote
de la Mancha."[2] Walter Allen in *The English Novel* opts for the
broad use of the term when he states: "if the word 'Picaresque' is
now stretched, as it commonly is, to mean any novel in which the
hero takes a journey whose course plunges him into all sorts, conditions, and classes of men, *The Pilgrim's Progress* is not so different
in form from the conventional picaresque novel."[3] An even broader
understanding of the term which renders it virtually useless is found
in Harold Child's remarks on *Humphry Clinker:* "In its way, this is
another picaresque story, insomuch as, during its progress, the
characters (who relate everything in letters to their friends), pursue
their travels in England and Scotland."[4] For many Hispanists such
statements on the picaresque are unacceptable, to say the least, and
it is obvious that more critical work on this genre is needed to overcome the cultural lag which exists especially among some scholars of
British and American literature.[5]

Robert Alter, in *Rogue's Progress: Studies in the Picaresque
Novel*, wrestles with the question of when and how to use the term
picaresque but does not really offer an answer. He believes that
critics ought to use the term with serious responsibility to the
historical phenomenon from which it derives, but he also allows
that there is sound intuition behind the broader applications of the
term.[6] In 1967 the distinguished Hispanist, Alexander A. Parker,
wrote his controversial study, *Literature and the Delinquent*, fulfill-
ing a definite need in Hispanic studies by stimulating other serious
critics to work on the picaresque. His provocative book stimulated
not only the attention but, at times, the ire of Hispanists and non-
Hispanists alike. For him the *picaro* is a delinquent similar to the

wayward youths of the 1960s. Parker is excessively restrictive in his use of the term, and unfortunately excludes *Lazarillo de Tormes* from the realm of the picaresque. He believes that this novel ''should be kept historically and thematically distinct from the picaresque *genre* proper, it must be given its due as the precursor.''[7] Stuart Miller's book, *The Picaresque Novel*,[8] is less provocative than Parker's. He attempts to formulate an ''ideal genre type'' with a number of coherent formal devices. Both Miller and Parker attempt to clarify the dilemma regarding the use of the term picaresque, but neither has the solution. Frohock is also aware of the problem, but offers no resolution.[9] It is no wonder that Eisenberg is so frustrated with the use of the term that he goes to another extreme, and proposes that it be dropped altogether from the vocabulary of literary criticism.[10] However, the term ''picaresque'' is here to stay, and it must be used with knowledge, care, and *mesure,* allowing for the study of picaresque models, later works influenced by these models, and the picaresque tradition as a whole.

Claudio Guillén and Ulrich Wicks in their thoughtful studies have extricated the picaresque from the mire of confusion caused by the extreme positions held by other critics. Guillén's essay, ''Toward a Definition of the Picaresque,''[11] is the most promising attempt to define the picaresque genre. His balanced and precise view of the picaresque allows for the inclusion of both strict and broad interpretations. In this essay Guillén suggests that considering the picaresque as an event only of the past is pedantic and erroneous. Treating the problem of defining the picaresque he says:

> it may be useful to distinguish between the following: the picaresque genre, first of all; a group of novels, secondly, that deserve to be called picaresque in the strict sense—usually in agreement with the original Spanish pattern; another group of novels, thirdly, which may be considered picaresque in a broader sense of the term only; and finally, a picaresque myth: an essential situation or significant structure derived from the novels themselves.[12]

In his discussion of what he calls picaresque novels in the strict sense, Guillén singles out eight features of the picaresque: (1) ''Our first feature . . . is a dynamic psycho-sociological situation, or series of situations, which can only be described—however briefly—in narrative fashion. It is, in this sense, a 'plot.' The *pícaro* is first of all an orphan. In the history of narrative forms, *Lazarillo de Tormes* represents the first significant appearance of the myth of the orphan. All later picaresque novels will build on this same highly suggestive situation.'' (2) ''The picaresque novel is a pseudoautobiography.'' (3) ''The narrator's view is . . . partial and prejudiced.'' (4) ''The total view of the *pícaro* is reflective, philosophical, critical on religious or moral grounds. As an autobiographer and an outsider, he collects broad conclusions—*il met le monde en question*.'' ·(5) ''There is a general stress on the material level of existence or of subsistence, on sordid facts, hunger, money.'' (6) ''The *pícaro* (though not always a servant of many masters) observes a number of collective conditions: social classes, professions, *caractères*, cities, and nations. . . . As a 'half-outsider,' his moral credentials are equivocal, though not his expert sense for fraud and deception.'' (7) ''The *pícaro* in his odyssey moves horizontally through space and vertically through society.'' (8) ''The novel is loosely episodic, strung together like a freight train and *apparently* with no other common link than the hero.''[13]

I cannot agree wholeheartedly with Guillén's view that the *pícaro* is an orphan because this presents us with a character type which, for me, is too strictly defined. What of those protagonists who are not orphans? Although one can sympathize with scholars who are confused or uncomfortable with the picaresque, I find Claudio Guillén's use of the term to be clear, manageable, and useful as a starting point. Not only does he give a precise view of the Spanish picaresque, he points out that a genre has stable features, but it also changes, as a precise influence on the work in progress, with the writer, the nation, and the period.[14] Guillén's fine study, however, is not the last word on the subject, and critical work still needs to be done on the picaresque, especially in the area of comparative literature.

Ulrich Wicks opts for a modal approach as a possible answer to the problem of the use of the term ''picaresque,'' and his study is helpful to the student of comparative literature.[15] Wicks uses Robert Scholes's theory of fictional modes as a starting point to develop his modal-generic approach to the picaresque. For Wicks the picaresque mode, which is located between satire and comedy on a spectrum that extends from satire to romance, presents a protagonist who endures a chaotic world, a world closer to ours than that portrayed by satire or romance. The modal perspective leads to a generic awareness, which in turn yields the specific attributes of genre. Wicks lists some aspects of the picaresque genre as: (1) dominance of the picaresque mode, (2) panoramic structure, (3) first-person point of view, (4) protagonist as *pícaro*, (5) *pícaro*-landscape relationship, (6) a vast gallery of human types, (7) implied parody of other fictional types (romance) and of the picaresque itself, and (8) certain basic themes and motifs. Wick's modal approach is especially useful because it is broad enough to account for larger fictional mixtures in any particular work and specific enough to account for a group of works that share a sufficient number of attributes which make them identifiable as belonging to a genre. The modal approach is also flexible. Although several modes may appear in a literary work, only one dominates. Another useful study on the picaresque which ought to be consulted is Fernando Lázaro Carreter's essay, "Para una revisión del concepto 'Novela Picaresca' " ("For a Revision of the Concept 'The Picaresque Novel' ").[16] Lázaro Carreter is correct when he states that it is necessary to consider the role of secondary works in order to understand the picaresque. One ought not consider the picaresque novel simply as an inert collection of works related by common characteristics. Instead it should be thought of as a dynamic process in which each work has a particular position regarding a certain poetic. Its writers are in the ambience of a genre, and no matter what modification they make, their creations profit from its poetics. Some other worthwhile studies to be consulted include Francisco Rico's *La novela picaresca y el punto de vista,* Christine J. Whitbourne's *Knaves and Swindlers,* Harry Sieber's *The Picaresque,* Richard Bjornson's *The Picaresque Hero,* and Peter N. Dunn's *The Spanish Picaresque Novel.*[17]

Many Hispanists and non-Hispanists in studying Spanish Golden Age picaresque fiction have first defined the *pícaro* then classified works as picaresque solely on the basis of whether the protagonists fit their definition. In my opinion, this approach—itself a source of confusion—has led some critics to believe that *Don Quixote* is picaresque because the protagonist appears to be a nonheroic traveler, the novel is episodic, and it contains realism and satire. What predominates in Spanish Golden Age picaresque fiction is *not* a strictly defined character type, whether rogue, delinquent, or orphan, but rather a particular novelistic technique. It is far more useful to base the discussion of the picaresque fiction on novelistic technique and themes rather than on a rigid *a priori* definition of a single character.

Picaresque fiction can be classified as empirical narrative whose primary allegiance is to reality rather than to *mythos,* a traditional story.[18] Its mode is mimetic rather than historical, because it depicts truth of sensation and environment rather than truth of fact. Picaresque fiction was probably influenced by *The Golden Ass* of Apuleius and the *Confessions* of Augustine, both mimetic first-person narratives which established the twofold pattern of the inward journey—the autobiography as apology and confession. The picaresque novel, which begins with *Lazarillo de Tormes,* emerges as a ''slice-of-life'' pseudoautobiography in which the *pícaro* an eye-witness narrator and frequently a social delinquent, is a *histor.* He is an inquirer and observer who examines the past, and presents the reader with his version of the truth. Because the perspective of the solitary narrator is partial and prejudiced, the picaresque novel does not attain Cervantes's more complex concept of reality which is based on several biased views rather than on a single one.[19] The recurrent themes of desire and disillusionment appear in the picaresque novel in varying degrees and in several ways. Generally speaking, many of the protagonist's actions and thoughts are motivated by the desire to improve his life, but after a series of failures or superficial successes, he is disillusioned (undeceived) because his life has not really improved. The narrator offers to the reader his experience, his observations, and his point of view as evidence of his thesis, namely, that life is filled with illusion and deceit. Sometimes the *pícaro* believes that his life has improved, but the reader, knowing that the protagonist is deceived, perceives the truth presented by the author.

The theme of *desengaño* (''disillusionment'')—the process by which man undeceives himself by waking to what he believes is a true awareness of things—was prevalent in Spanish literature of the 1600s, especially in the picaresque novel and the drama.[20] The best example of the theme is in the picaresque novel, *Guzmán de Alfarache,* which A. A. Parker believes satisfied the demands of the Counter-Reformation, since it was realistic literature and more truthful and responsible than the idealistic literature of that period. *Guzmán* served the ends of truth because it illustrated explicitly the doctrines of sin, repentance, and salvation through the protagonist who goes in search of the love of the world only to land in infamy.

Parker believes the heroes of romance were in this way replaced by a *pícaro*, Guzmán, a thief and galley slave who in the end wins through to regeneration.[21] In *Lazarillo de Tormes*, the treatment of the disillusionment theme and the narrator's perception of the world are less dogmatic and more subtle than in *Guzmán de Alfarache* and some other picaresque works of seventeeth-century Spain.

In *Lazarillo de Tormes* the protagonist/narrator gives the reader an eyewitness account of his life. The protagonist in this pseudo-success story has a desire to improve his lot, but after combatting adverse fortune and suffering a series of misfortunes, his life really has not improved. This novel, second in popularity to *Don Quixote* in Spanish literature, is artistically written with regard to form, style, and ideas; it stands as the model for the picaresque novel in Spain.

Chapter Two
Editions

In 1554, three separate editions of *La vida de Lazarillo de Tormes y de sus fortunas y adversidades* appeared: one was published by Juan de Junta in Burgos; one by Martín Nucio in Antwerp; and one by Salcedo in Alcalá de Henares.[1] The three 1554 editions contain numerous variants, and the problems of authenticity and the relationships among them continue to puzzle critics. There is mention of earlier editions, but none is extant. Brunet believed that there was a 1553 edition published in Antwerp;[2] Bonilla y San Martín spoke of one published outside of Spain in 1550;[3] Viardot thought there was a 1538 edition;[4] and finally Rumeau, who studied the problems regarding the early editions, denied that there ever existed an earlier edition published before 1554.[5] Although Rumeau's arguments are convincing, the questions regarding the date of composition and the enigma of the 1554 editions still draw the interest of numerous critics.

The first scholarly study of the three 1554 editions was done by Morel-Fatio, who came to the conclusion that the Burgos edition was the *princeps;* next came the Flemish edition, which for him was an imitation of the Burgos, and finally the Alcalá.[6] The Alcalá edition contains two important notices: one says it is a second printing with additions and corrections, and the other states that the work was finished 26 February 1554. It is difficult to believe that in a period of just fifty-six days into the year the printer in Alcalá could have obtained and used either of the other two 1554 editions. Foulché-Delbosc believes that the three 1554 editions appeared in this order: the Alcalá, the Burgos, then the Antwerp. They in turn were preceded by the *princeps* which was probably the 1553 edition mentioned by Brunet. The Alcalá differs from the other two editions with its inclusion of six brief interpolations of some 2,000 words which differ from the style of the novel and appear to be spurious.[7] The general opinion now is that the changes in the Alcalá edition are apocryphal. They were probably corrections and additions made by Salcedo himself. In 1555 Simón, a resident of Antwerp, reedited the work; this edition unfortunately was included with the rest on the infamous Index of 1559. Years later, in the meticulous edition of Juan López Velasco, there was an allusion to the diffusion of the book outside of Spain. However, it is not known in which countries the *Lazarillo* was published.

The problems of the numerous variants and the affiliation of the three 1554 texts were first studied in a scientific way by Alfredo Cavaliere and then by José Caso González, Francisco Rico, and Alberto Blecua.[8] For all practical purposes the issue of the 1554 editions has been resolved. Alfredo Cavaliere's exhaustive study of the 1554 texts is well documented and convincing. He uses the Lachmann genealogical method which holds that texts having a common error have a common ancestor from which they derive the common error, and texts having common agreement have a common ancestor from which they derive their common agreement. Cavaliere postulates that there was a prototype for the three 1554 editions which is now lost and that the most faithful of the 1554 editions is the Burgos. He believes that the Alcalá is fundamentally different from the Burgos, and that the Antwerp contains many forms of the Burgos and some of the Alcalá. Cavaliere hypothesizes that the Burgos is the most reliable and archaic, that the Antwerp is closer to the Burgos than the Alcalá, which is fundamentally different from the other two, and that the Alcalá is marred by the interpolations. His theories seem irrefutable.

Caso González, Francisco Rico, and Alberto Blecua are among the recent critics who have studied the variants of the three 1554 editions and their relationships to one another. They too have come to the conclusion that there existed one or more previous editions. Francisco Rico accepts Cavaliere's theory that there exists a lost edition on which the others are based and that it was probably published not much before 1554.[9] José Caso González rejects Cavaliere's theory as too simple, and holds that there were several lost editions and thus no single one from which the others were derived. After studying carefully all of the existing known editions of the sixteenth century, he concluded that it was useless to speak of or try to reconstruct an original text since there were two families of manuscripts. One is reflected in the Burgos edition which has one or more intermediaries between it and the original. The Antwerp and the Alcalá could stem from a common prototype which branched off into two directions. Caso believes that Salcedo knew of a prior edition, and that it was neither the Burgos nor the 1554 Antwerp edition. Later Caso modified his theories and concluded that around 1550 Martín Nucio asked for and received imperial privilege to edit the *Lazarillo de Tormes*.[10] This is the book which probably was later owned by the Duque de T'Serclaes, and it was perhaps also one of those that the Marqués de Jerez de los Caballeros gave to booksellers between 1902 and 1911. Martín Nucio reedited the novel after having corrected it in 1553. No one has seen it, but Caso believes that Brunet could be right in believing that it existed. At about the same time, in Alcalá de Henares, this book was reedited by Salcedo, who in turn corrected and added to the text of 1550, and in addition had before him another manuscript. Caso also believes that the first editon of the *Lazarillo* underwent modifications. There was one slight modification in the Antwerp 1554 edition; the Burgos was also slightly changed with new additions and errors; and the third and most important was the Alcalá, which was modified more than the rest.

Alberto Blecua offers a resolution to the problems surrounding the three 1554 editions based on their punctuation. He studied carefully the three editions and found that their punctuation is almost identical, leading him to conclude that the three texts derived from a common printing and not from manuscripts.[11] His schema, which corresponds to Cavaliere's and Rico's proposals, is as follows.

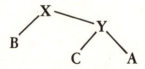

Blecua believes that there existed a lost edition (X) from which the Burgos (B) is derived and a printed text (Y) which gave rise to the Antwerp (C) and Alcalá (A) editions. The punctuation of (A) and (B) is faithful to the archetype. They retain the same errors, but (C) corrects the errors. The Alcalá copies an edition (Y) and the interpolations were probably done by Salcedo without any manuscript whatsoever. Blecua also believes that the later Simón, Milan editions, and almost certainly the Velasco edition, are from the (C) Antwerp text. He does not deny the possibility that there were more editions which have been lost, that there may exist other branches of manuscripts, or that X could derive from an earlier edition.

The fact that there were three editions published in 1554 suggests that the book was a considerable success, but Blecua thinks that there is no reason to believe that the *Lazarillo* was published as early as 1525, as Cavaliere suggested. For Blecua the *Lazarillo* must have been published in 1553, or 1552, not before. There were certainly two lost editions; however, the existence of other editions before 1554 has to this day not been demonstrated. Blecua's conclusions regarding the mystery of the three 1554 texts are reasonable and well founded; however the date of the composition of the *Lazarillo* continues to elicit critical discussion.

When was this book written? How many editions of the archetype(s) exist? These are questions which remain unanswered. Some critics turn to the book itself for internal evidence to substantiate their theories regarding date of publication. They take the historical matters mentioned in the novel and the chronological time of the protagonist literally, and substantiate their theories accordingly. The two most important historical references mentioned in the novel are the *Cortes* ("Parliament") of Toledo convened by Charles V and the Battle of Los Gelves. The allusion to the Parliament comes at the end of the book when the adult Lázaro says: "This was the same year that our victorious Emperor entered this famous city of Toledo and convened the Parliament, and there were grand festivities, as Your Grace must have heard."

The Parliament to which Lázaro refers could have taken place in Toledo in 1525, or in 1538-39. The supporting evidence for the 1525 date is that Charles V could well have been described as victorious since he defeated the French at Pavia in 1525, and returned to Madrid with his prisoner Francis I, the king of France.[12] The internal chronological evidence to support this theory would be that Lazarillo was eight years old when his father died fighting Moors at the Battle of Los Gelves (which these critics date at 1510). Lázaro at the end of the book is a town crier and gets married when he is about twenty-three years old. This makes for a credible story. In the third chapter Lazarillo describes how he used to lie awake suffering from hunger, and he compares this suffering to the *cuidados del rey de Francia* ("troubles of the king of France"), which would make sense especially if the allusion refers to Francis I, prisoner in Madrid until February 1526. However, this may simply be an idiomatic expression popular at that time which refers to his own suffering rather than to an historical fact.

On the other hand the Parliament could have been convened in
1538–39, and the Battle at Los Gelves could well have taken place in
1520. In accordance with this series of events, Lázaro at the end of
the novel would be some twenty-six years old, also an acceptable age
for the protagonist. A third possibility would be the battle in 1520,
and the Parliament in 1538–39, which would make Lázaro about
thirty-six years old, a view that is less likely but nevertheless realistic.

There is no decisive evidence for or against either date for the
Parliament. Some believe that the Parliament of 1538–39 could not
have been very festive. Charles V had just signed the Treaty of Nice
which was not favorable for Spain, and furthermore the empress
had died during childbirth. There was no victory to celebrate and
the Battle of Los Gelves of 1520 was not as important to Spain as the
first battle there in 1510. In fact, Padre Mariana in the *Sumario*
("Summary") of 1520 does not even mention the later expedition. [13] No matter which date one prefers for the Parliament,
nothing is proved concerning the date of composition, nor does it
alter a great deal the internal chronology of the protagonist. If one
chooses the 1525 date, that would only confirm that the novel was
written after this date. The precise date would still be unknown.
The same is true for the 1538–39 date. Neither date for the Battle of
Los Gelves alters the dating of composition in a significant way.

Since critics have not been able to quench their curiosity using the
date of the Parliament, the Battle of Los Gelves, and other internal
historical evidence, they have turned to the intellectual and social
atmosphere at the time of so-called publication to support their
theses. Manuel J. Asensio[14] is convinced that only in 1525 could
Charles V have been considered victorious as described in the novel.
The 1525 date reflects, for him, the social, religious, and ideological
ambience of Toledo. He considers the book to be tied to the Erasmian polemic, and the author an illuminist of the Valdés circle.
This circle was related to the duke of Escalona, who died in 1529,
and who may be alluded to in the text. Joseph V. Ricapito is convinced by Asensio's arguments that the book pertained to the Erasmian polemic, and for him the earlier date is more plausible. [15]

The 1525 date may suit the internal chronology of the book better, but it still does not prove that the Parliament was held in 1525.
Lazarillo lost his father at eight years old[16] and was given to the
blind man as a guide when his brother began to walk. He served the
Priest of the Order of Mercy eight days, then he spent eight months

with the Pardoner, and later four years with the Chaplain. Up to this point the chronological date would be 1520 or 1521. The protagonist later spends a brief time with the Constable, becomes a town crier, and marries the mistress of the Archpriest. After this takes place he writes his pseudoautobiography, the date of which could easily have been 1525–26. The system of chronology lends credence to those who believe that the *Lazarillo de Tormes* was written ten to twenty years before the first known edition.

No matter which date for the Parliament we choose, the problem of dating the composition remains. Again, if one is literal minded, either date leaves enough time to create the novel. Since it is not known who the author was nor the date of the Parliament, it is extremely difficult to hazard a guess as to date of composition. This fact still has not silenced some critics, who have turned elsewhere in the novel for evidence. Asensio and Martín de Riquer stress the importance of the sentence, "This was the same year that our victorious emperor entered this famous city of Toledo and held his Parliament here; there were great festivities as Your Grace no doubt has heard." They believe that Parliament was held in 1525, and that the date of composition came a little later. Marcel Bataillon and Francisco Márquez Villanueva hold that the date of the work is close to the date of the first publication, 1554, because the literary perspective suits that of *El Abencerraje* and other contemporary pieces. Bataillon sees a reflection of the socioeconomic environment of the 1540s with its abundance of beggars and vagabonds in the cities, which gave rise to a decree in 1543. This decree may be alluded to in the third chapter. Lazarillo, while in the service of the Squire of Toledo, says: "since this year there was such a shortage of bread, the City Hall ordered all poor foreigners to leave the city." Bataillon believes that the novel reflects the 1540–50 decade because of the movement against beggars and vagabonds during this period which culminated with the decree of 1543, which banned beggars from Toledo because of the drought that the city suffered. The social situation may be reflected in the statements made by Lazarillo about the decree and the drought, and it may be related to the lack of charity the protagonist finds in Toledo. Sentences like "You-good-for-nothing scoundrel. Go on, go find a master and get a job," tend to make one believe that some Toledans thought there were some jobs about and that Lazarillo ought to get one. Toledo was not a city without work for drifters if one were to take this sentence literally. In my opinion, the author created a fictitious ambience of hardship for Lazarillo for artistic rather than historical purposes. Without the artistic ambience the novel would lose its impact, plot, and structure, and the protagonist, his motives. The environment, realistic as it may be, is housed in a fictitious account presented by a fictitious narrator.

There are those critics who base their theories regarding the date of composition on the ideology which they think is reflected in the novel. Asensio believes that the social, religious, and ideological problems common to Toledo and Escalona were those dealt with by the Parliament of 1525: vagrancy, discontent with the practices of the Church, the precarious position of poor nobles—all of which are reflected in the novel.[17] He believes that the text portrays five clergymen as social parasites and that the focus on them must be related to the socio-religious intent of the author. Joseph Ricapito argues that the book pertains to the Erasmian polemic, and that the religious and social problems treated in the novel are similar to those found in the works of Alfonso de Valdés. The *Lazarillo* does reflect most probably the ideology and social situation of its time, but solid evidence necessary to pinpoint "its" time is lacking. The internal evidence is couched in fiction, and is not solid enough to date the work. Thus the only avenue left is to look for evidence outside of the novel, documents that allude to the work, which brings us full circle to the strange and profound silence regarding the work and its author. The first references to the work which can be taken seriously come after 1554. Since there are no firm data on which to date the *Lazarillo de Tormes*, Blecua concludes, as I do, that the date of composition is close to that of publication. This would explain the absence of allusions, and the literary development of autobiography, and the Erasmian polemic taking place in the 1550s.[18]

In light of the available evidence one can conclude that there is one fact which is indisputable: three editions of the novel were published in 1554. It is improbable that the book was published some twenty to thirty years previous to this date. There remain unanswered questions. Were there editions previous to 1554, which were lost, and did three editions suddenly appear followed by a second part published in 1555? If an archetype does exist, it was probably written in 1553; this would explain the silence. Finally, if manuscripts had been circulating since 1530, as some critics claim, how was the book published during the time when the Inquisition was especially vigilant? The enormous success of this book leads one to suppose that the composition and the first publication of the novel were not much before 1554. This is not a book about which people could have been silent for long.

Chapter Three
Continuations and Early Translations

After the initial success of the *Lazarillo de Tormes* there was a puzzling drop in its popularity in the second half of the century which coincides, as A. Rumeau points out, with the reign of Philip II.[1] During the second half of the century the book was published only five times: in Madrid (1573); Tarragona (1586); Milan (1587); Antwerp (1595); and Bergamo (1597). The first continuation of the novel, the anonymous *Second Part of Lazarillo de Tormes,* was published by Martín Nucio and Guillermo Simón in Antwerp in 1555, and was reprinted in Milan in 1587 and 1615. It has almost nothing in common with the picaresque and was not popular in Spain. Indeed, it does not reappear in Spain until 1844. In the *Second Part* Lázaro enlists in the army and is shipwrecked in North Africa. His belly is so filled with wine that there is no room for water to enter, and thus he does not drown. Lázaro takes his sword and does battle with some tuna fish. In the end he is surrounded by them. He is saved when he himself is turned into a tuna fish. He then teaches the fish swordsmanship, and after several amusing adventures he is appointed an officer of their army. Lázaro is later captured by Spanish fishermen who remove his skin and discover that he is a human being. This allegorical story was probably influenced by Apuleius's *Golden Ass,* and Villalón's *The Dialogue of Transformations* and *El Crotalón.* Although the *Second Part* alludes to Lázaro's previous life and continues the themes of fortune and adversity, it is more in the satirical tradition of the *Golden Ass* and the tales of Lucian than the picaresque genre.

Lazarillo de Tormes Castigado

In the 1550s, the Spanish Inquisition became involved in the censure of books, and since *Lazarillo de Tormes* was considered dangerous to the faith and to morals, it was one of the first placed on the infamous "Index," *Cathalogus librorum qui prohibentur* (Catalog of Prohibited Books, 1559). But Lázaro's story could not be completely suppressed. Some twelve years later the prohibition was lifted, and Juan López Velasco received permission to publish the 1573 censored edition, *Lazarillo de Tormes castigado* (*Lazarillo de Tormes Expurgated*) which appeared in Madrid. Guillén points out that the Antwerp original, not the Burgos or the Alcalá, was the basis of this edition.[2] Chapters 4 and 5 of the original which deal with the Monk and the Pardoner are omitted and several observations on the clergy and court customs were removed. The episodes of the Priest and the Archpriest, however, remain intact.[3] The prohibition of Spanish editions probably stimulated foreigners to publish the novel which appeared again in Antwerp in 1602. Other Spanish editions appear soon after the ban was lifted, for example in Tarragona (1586) and Valladolid (1603).[4]

La Segunda Parte de Lazarillo de Tormes

Juan de Luna, a native Toledan, was persecuted by the Inquisition at Zaragoza before going to Paris where he became an interpreter and teacher of Spanish. He published the *Second Part of Lazarillo de Tormes* there in 1620.[5] He resented the treatment that he received in Spain and used the prologue of his novel as a device to plead for justice and tolerance, which he believed had been denied him. In the prologue he relates a fable about a farmer who has pears that are so famous that an Inquisitor wants to try some. When the farmer hears of the Inquisitor's interest he becomes so fearful that he uproots the pear tree and sends it off hoping to avoid a visit from the Inquisitor.

Luna builds on the previous *Second Part of Lazarillo de Tormes* by denying its veracity and attempting to set the record straight. He says that he will give a true account of Lázaro's further adventures and misfortunes as they were told him by his great-grandmother and as they were preserved in the "Chronicles" of Toledo. Luna's story has Lázaro embark for a battle against the North Africans. He is shipwrecked and remains only a short while in the sea where he discovers a treasure chest which he salvages by tying a cord to his leg and rising to the surface. Some greedy fishermen rescue Lázaro and unwittingly cut loose the treasure. When they learn what they have done, they decide to derive some profit from Lázaro and exhibit him in a tank of water, as a sea monster. He is displayed around the country and in one of his aquatic performances is almost drowned. He escapes from his impressarios and undergoes a series of picaresquelike adventures, clashing with police and meeting low-life characters. He is deceived and deceives. Lázaro brings suit against his wife and the Archpriest, then meets a hermit and decides to join him. Soon after, the hermit dies, and Lázaro discovers that he had been deceived by the hermit's appearance. The hypocritical hermit had amassed a fortune from the alms of pilgrims. After discovering the wealth, Lázaro decides to marry the hermit's "widow." He is fooled once again. What he takes to be a form of a ceremony turns out to be a series of tortures from which he gladly escapes. In the end Lázaro, unlike his cynical predecessor, adopts an ascetic posture and resigns himself to a life of suffering and poverty. Luna ends the narrative by stating that he has written it as it was told to him by his great-grandmother, without adding or omitting anything.

The original *Lazarillo de Tormes* apparently appealed to Luna for its critical stance on a corrupt society. However, although there are links with the original, in the reappearance, for instance, of the Squire, Wife, and Archpriest, Luna's protagonist differs from the earlier one. Lazarillo learns how to survive in a corrupt society while Luna's Lázaro manipulates, outwits, and disgraces. The original protagonist is a cynic, Luna's an ascetic. Some critics believe that Luna's version is out of character with the original *Lazarillo de Tormes* and that he failed to understand its subtlety and complexity,[6] while others consider his book an ingenious interpretation of the themes and technique of the first novel.[7] In England, a translation of Luna's *Second Part,* entitled *The Pursuit of the History of Lazarillo de Tormes,* was popular in the seventeenth century. This book was later reprinted as *The Witty Spaniard* and published together with an anonymous sequel, *The Life and Death of Young Lazarillo.*[8] Paul Keufuss translated Luna's work into German in 1653, and published it together with the *Lazarillo de Tormes* of 1617.

Lazarillo de Manzanares

In 1620 *Lazarillo de Manzanares,* by Juan Cortés de Tolosa, was published together with five other novels in Madrid. The protagonist of this narrative is born in Madrid. His parents are like Pablos's in *El Buscón*. His father is a thief who is in jail for trying to hang his mother who is supected of being a witch. Lazarillo is sent to study at Alcalá, where he serves a pastry cook and helps her to make pies from dead horses. Misfortune strikes. The cook, who is his mistress, presents him with a baby, and his mother is taken prisoner by the Inquisition. His next master is a one-eyed sacristan whose deceiving wife keeps Lazarillo busy running errands. In Madrid again, the protagonist serves a ruffian and later becomes a partner at cheating a hermit. He and the hermit travel for several years through Spain, and Lazarillo finds his mother, part of an auto-de-fé, in Toledo. After the hermit's death Lazarillo strikes up a relationship with a young gentleman of Seville, then takes to begging, and finally serves as a tutor to the nephews of a canon. The story ends with a rich gentleman sending him to Mexico in one of his ships.

The book is written in the first person and starts in a manner similar to the original, addressing "Your Grace." Part of the story is derived from *El Buscón*. Like Pablos, Lazarillo begins with student life and ends up on a ship heading for the Americas. The witchcraft of the mother and the motif of the pastry also suggests influence of the *Buscón*. *Lazarillo de Manzanares* simply strings adventures together and has neither the continuity nor the well-developed protagonist of the original.

The First Translations

By 1595 only seven Spanish editions of *Lazarillo de Tormes* had appeared, but within the next eight years the book was reprinted no less than ten times.[9] The early translations of the novel served as a catalyst for French, English, German, and Italian writers who were influenced by it.

The first French translation appeared in Lyons in 1560, and was reprinted in Paris in 1561. This translation adds a chapter that appeared in the *Second Part* of Antwerp in 1555. It deals with Lázaro's friendship with some Germans who are in love with wine. A bilingual edition was published in 1660, and an imitation in French verse in 1653. The first Italian version was published in 1608, signed by a Oiluigi Izzortesse; others appeared in Venice in 1622, 1635, and 1636.[10] The oldest German version was translated in Breslau in 1614; the first published texts appeared in Augsburg in 1617 and 1627. There were four different English translations during the sixteenth century. The most popular was David Rowland's version of 1568; others followed in 1576, 1586, 1596, 1624, and 1631. The Dutch translations were published in Antwerp in 1579, Delft in 1609, Utrecht in 1654, and Amsterdam in 1669. Gaspar Ens published a Latin translation based on the 1617 German text in Cologne, 1623.

The translations were adapted and assimilated according to the literary conventions and world views of the country and the time. Some translators thought the novel was a jest book; others stereotyped the figures in the novel and believed that the book contained instructive and accurate descriptions of society. Jean Saugrain, who rendered it into French in 1560, says on the title page that the book is "highly amusing and delightful" and contains "marvelous things, terrible adventures . . . notable deeds and jests." The Augsburg German translator of *Lazarillo de Tormes* thinks of it as a collection of jokes in the literary tradition of *Till Eulenspiegel.* Rowland's dedication states that the reader will learn about "the nature and disposition of sundrie Spaniards," while a later French translation asserts that "all Spaniards are the same and would rather die of hunger than take up a trade."[11] The translators were only human and, like others, regarded foreigners as stereotypes. The negative image of Spaniards in England and France was heightened by the hostilities between these countries and the Hapsburg kingdom. For all that, *Lazarillo de Tormes* has had a long and sustained impact on world literature. Its influence on narrative technique, character development, and world view in the novel is attested both in and out of Spain.[12]

Chapter Four
Authorship

Judging by the number of editions that appear in 1554, and those which quickly followed both in and out of Spain, the book was a success right from the start. Although, as we have seen, many critics have studied the problem of editions, they have been equally absorbed by the question of the anonymity of the novel. Neither mystery has yet been resolved. The search for a *princeps* edition and for the author has stimulated critics over the ages to hypothesize and offer interesting theories. A second-rate work could easily have been forgotten, but it is difficult, if not impossible, to relegate such an excellent and popular novel to anonymity. Thus the polemic surrounding the authorship which started over three hundred years ago continues to thrive and inspire scholarship. The approaches and theories of the critics naturally contain biases and preferences which are affected by the epoch in which they write. They are for the most part perspicuous and convincing, some are even well founded, but the anonymity of the original author remains intact and continues to this day to draw the interest of the critics.

The anonymity of this popular book stimulated interest and speculation soon after the first known publication date. The first two candidates for the authorship of the novel are Fray Juan de Ortega, a Hieronymite elected general of his Order in 1552 and 1555, and Diego Hurtado de Mendoza, a distinguished noble who could have written the work when a student in Salamanca.

Fray José de Sigüenza, a Hieronymite historian, suggested in 1605 that Juan de Ortega was the author. He states that a rough draft of the *Lazarillo de Tormes* was found in Ortega's cell at the time of his death.[1] This is really scanty evidence since the draft may or may not have been Ortega's, and even if it were his, it could have been a copy of the original or another edition. While the attribution of the book to Ortega has been supported by some important scholars,[2] there are also some noted critics who reject this theory, principally Manuel J. Asensio and Joseph H. Silverman.[3]

In 1607, Valerius Andreas Texandrus attributed the *Lazarillo de Tormes* to Diego Hurtado de Mendoza.[4] The attribution was

repeated one year later by Andreas Schott[5] and in 1624,[6] by Tomás
Tamayo de Vargas. Their arguments, which are based on hearsay
and not substantiated by facts, are unconvincing. The list of critics
who believe that Mendoza could be the author of *Lazarillo de
Tormes* is substantial.[7] One of his principal defenders is González
Palencia who argues that Valerius Andreas's information is trust-
worthy, that Mendoza's anticlerical attitude and his style of writing
is suited to the *Lazarillo de Tormes*, and that his silence regarding
the authorship makes sense, for at the time of its publication he was
out of favor with the king. Neither Juan Díaz Hidalgo, the first
editor of Mendoza's *Poesías* (Madrid, 1610) nor Baltasar de Zúñiga
who wrote a biography (1627) of Mendoza mention him as the
author of *Lazarillo de Tormes*. They believe that it was improbable
that an aristocrat, probably a student in Salamanca at the time the
book was supposed to have been written, would treat such lowly
matter as is found in the novel in such a bitter way. They also note
the differences in style between the *Lazarillo de Tormes* and Mendoza's other works.

In addition to Ortega and Mendoza as possible authors of the
Lazarillo de Tormes, the list of candidates includes Lope de Rueda,
a *pregonero* ("town crier") from Toledo; Sebastián de Horozco,
author of *Refranes glosados* (*Glossed Proverbs*); the humanist
Hernán Núñez; Pedro de Rhúa; and the Erasmians, Juan and
Alfonso Valdés.

Fonger de Haan considered the *Lazarillo de Tormes* literally to be
an autobiography of Lope de Rueda who was town crier of Toledo in
1538; Fred Abrams, basing his arguments on the Burgos text as the
princeps and some biographical coincidences, supports this theory.[8]
Yet there is no concrete data which makes this view credible.

Sebastián de Horozco's candidacy, proposed originally by José
María Asensio y Toledo, has been supported by Julio Cejador y
Frauca and most recently by F. Márquez Villanueva.[9] Asensio and
Cejador y Frauca base their arguments on similarity of style and content. Asensio points out a scene of a play by Horozco in which there
is a blind man and his *mozo* ("servant") called Lazarillo. He compares this scene with the pillar incident in *Lazarillo de Tormes*. In
Horozco's work Lazarillo plays a tricks on his blind master, causing
him to bump into a corner, and he says: "You smelled the bacon,
how is it that you did not smell the corner?" In her discussion of this
scene María Rosa Lida de Malkiel observes that without the novel,

Horozco's scene would be almost incomprehensible. [10] There is an undeniable similarity between Horozco's scene and the incident in the novel, but the basis for both of them was folklore, common property of all Spaniards. Márquez Villanueva supports Horozco's candidacy with more convincing arguments. He finds that in Horozco's work there are blind men, squires, and monks presented in a manner similar to that of the novel, and almost all of the proverbs in the novel are found in Horozco's *Glossed Proverbs*. There is a striking similarity between the proverbs and the material in *Lazarillo de Tormes*, but the weakness in Márquez Villanueva's arguments is that Horozco did not create the material himself; he collected the proverbs which were, in effect, part of the linguistic cultural patrimony of Spain. In his consideration of historical data, Márquez Villanueva notes that Horozco knew Salamanca and Toledo well, and that Juan de Junta, who later in 1554 would publish the Burgos edition of *Lazarillo de Tormes*, published anonymously Horozco's *Libro del número septenario*. Márquez Villanueva's theories are well documented and somewhat convincing, but one must question why Horozco's authorship was kept a secret and why there is such a great difference between his style and that of the novel. Rumeau's candidate, Hernán de Núñez, and Marasso's Pedro de Rhúa ought to be dismissed because of the scanty evidence and weak arguments used to support them.

There are, then, a number of critics who have attempted unsatisfactorily to identify *who* the author of *Lazarillo de Tormes* was. There are others who have tried to establish the identity of the author by determining *what* he was. Using the text of the novel, its themes, and its use of language, some critics theorize about the author's religious and ideological beliefs. Morel-Fatio initiated the theory that the author had Erasmian inclinations, basing his arguments on the anticlericalism in the novel. [11] The renowned specialist on the influence of Erasmus in Spain, Marcel Bataillon, takes issue with this argument. He believes that the author's anticlericalism is more a continuation of the trend started in the Middle Ages than an expression of his epoch. Speaking of the anticlericalism in the work, he says that the author adds nothing new to the medieval tradition. The priest of Maqueda is reproached for his lack of charity and the chaplain for his life which lacked austerity. Bataillon holds that this criticism of the clerics does not differ from the satire found in the *fabliaux* ("fables"). For him Erasmian satire is different in that it reproaches the clergy not for their bad life-style but for their beliefs.[12] In spite of the weight of Bataillon's conclusions, the theory that the author was an Erasmian was revived by Manuel J. Asensio and continues to be supported by other critics, including Joseph Ricapito.[13] There are other scholars, notably Américo Castro, who, noting the author's attitudes on religion, ecclesiastics, and honor, conclude that he was a *marginado* ("marginal person") and probably a *converso* ("convert"),[14] a theory which also continues to draw support.

It is evident that the author wished to remain anonymous and certainly succeeded in doing so. This anonymity and the reasons for it persist in intriguing critics. Some hypothesize that it would have been imprudent for the author to identify himself either because of the content of the novel, especially the denigrating material concerning the Church, or because of his socio-religious position.[15] No one really knows for sure what the author's position in society was, but the mystery has led to speculation which is thought-provoking.

Américo Castro studies the language and themes of the text to discover the author's attitude regarding religion, the clergy, and honor and concludes that the author probably was a New Christian.[16] For Guillén, it is the alienation, the ruthless lucidity, and the rediscovery of values which lead him to conclude that the author was a New Christian or of a similar mentality.[17] Some of the language in the novel that Castro refers to is of Judeo-Moslem origin, but that language, like the folklore, was the patrimony of Spain and was widely used by converts and Christians alike. It is true that Christ is not mentioned in the novel and that there are numerous references to the Old Testament, but this is not conclusive proof that the writer was a New Christian. The Judeo-Moslem, New Christian culture pervaded Spain and left its imprint on both Christian and non-Christian, and there were people from both groups who were alienated and disenfranchised.

The author does not really fit in the orthodox culture of Spain, and he definitely was a bold, cultured, and witty person given to irony. There are some episodes in the novel which denigrated the officials and practices of the Church. Of the nine masters that Lazarillo serves, five are connected with religion in one way or another, and none is presented in an ideal fashion. Does this mean that the author was an Erasmian reformer? This is a question which ought to be dealt with but is difficult to answer. The material in the novel,

which may be Erasmian, including the author's treatment of
religion, is shrouded more by irony than by satire, and thus it is
difficult to come to a definite conclusion. The basic difference between irony and satire is that satire, as Northrup Frye says, is militant irony and its moral standards are relatively clear.[18] Because of
the irony which pervades *Lazarillo de Tormes* from beginning to
end, the reader is never certain what the author's attitude is nor
what the reader's is supposed to be. The moral attitude is suppressed by the irony which makes the novel more artistically subtle
and elusive than other picaresque novels, such as *Guzmán de
Alfarache* and *El Buscón*. The realism in the book, however, is expressed in such a way as to make the reader view Spanish society in
an unorthodox, perhaps even heterodoxical way, but the novel does
not go so far as to beg the question of reform. The author is not
simply a reformer with a cause. The narrative technique is more artistic and subtle than that of an overt reformer. Thus for those who
insist that Erasmians were simply reformers, one would have to conclude that the author is not of that school of thought. However, if
one holds that not all Erasmians were simple reformers, then considering the style and content of *Lazarillo de Tormes*, it is probable
that the author was a somewhat heterodoxical humanist, an Erasmian, or one influenced by that persuasion.

América Castro does not believe that anticlericalism alone can
lead one to conclude that the author was an Erasmian; however, he
believes that the attitudes of the Squire in chapter 3 suggest a contact with Erasmian thought.[19] For him the Squire cultivates a certain
spirit of nobility and because of his sense of aristocracy considers
himself to be "enlightened." Interior nobility is enough for the
Squire; it is Utopia for him. For Castro, the Squire's sense of nobility reflects Erasmian thought; however, the simple anticlericalism of
the novel has nothing to do with this school of philosophy.[20]

While the two renowned scholars América Castro and Marcel
Bataillon do not believe that *Lazarillo de Tormes* was written by an
Erasmian, there are other noted scholars who disagree. The next
major critic after Morel-Fatio to hold that the author was an Erasmian was Manuel J. Asensio.[21] This distinguished critic is convinced
that the novel was written during the time of the imprisonment of
Francis I; he identifies the duke of Escalona, mentioned in *tratado* I,
as Diego López Pacheco who used to meet the *alumbrados* ("il-
luminated ones"), including Juan de Valdés himself or a member

of his circle. Asensio's study is impressive, and he has demonstrated convincingly that the author did intend to criticize religious practices of the time. Lazarillo's five masters who are connected with religion in one way or another occupy a great part of the novel and are soundly criticized. Asensio's arguments are even more convincing when one remembers that the masters who have no contact with religion, the Bailiff and the Painter of tambourines, are merely mentioned and are not of great importance. The Blind Man does have some contact with religious practices, and in the third chapter the narrator mentions God and refers to His grand scheme. Almost all of the characters in the book, and especially the Squire, are social parasites with the clergy at the forefront. Asensio considers Juan de Valdés to be the author of *Lazarillo de Tormes* and bases his arguments on the similarity of the novel to the ideas, the realism, the unadorned style, and the popular material found in Valdés's *Diálogo de la lengua* (*Dialogue of Language*). He also sees a similarity in Valdés's condemnation of materialism and lack of charity in his *Diálogo de la doctrina cristiana* (*Dialogue of Christian Doctrine*).[22] Asensio's investigation of the *Cortes* ("Parliament") of 1525 is impressive, and his study of the religious intention and style of the author is well founded. Nevertheless, it is difficult to accept Juan de Valdés as the author of *Lazarillo de Tormes*. It is true that Juan de Valdés would have shared many of the ideals and ideas that the book contains. It is also evident that the author was a learned humanist who was independent in spirit and artistically creative. Given the themes, the style, and the critical attitude of the author he was in all probability an Erasmian.[23] Francisco Rico's thoughts on this matter are equally sound. He believes we should not reject the possibility of Erasmian thought in the novel.[24] If the publication date is around 1550, one could almost be sure of Erasmian influence. Moreover, the criticism in the novel of the use of honor and the vulgar misuse of religion make one think that the author is similar to a number of enlightened Christians of that era, such as Juan de Mena, Álvarez Gato, and Luis Vives.

Nevertheless, the attribution of the novel to Juan de Valdés is difficult to accept, although it is likely that the author had contact with the Valdesian ideology. In my opinion the attitude of the protagonist represented in the novel is that of a philosophical skeptic and may well be that of an Erasmian.[25] Joseph Ricapito in his recent edition of *Lazarillo de Tormes* studies the possibility of the author's being an Erasmian, and reopens the case for Alfonso de Valdés as the author. Ricapito accepts Asensio's argument for the 1525 date of the Parliament but rejects Juan de Valdés as the author of the novel, because the author of *Lazarillo de Tormes* had a greater historical and social awareness than Juan de Valdés. Many of the opinions in the novel were no doubt shared by Juan de Valdés, but his work lacks the mordacity of the author as well as the ambiguity and irony which are found in the novel.[26] Of course without precise data the case for or against Juan de Valdés cannot be proved.

Ricapito studies carefully the possible attribution of the novel to someone in the Valdesian circle and puts forth Alfonso de Valdés as the possible author. He studies Alfonso's close relationship to Charles V, his important position in the court, and his relationship with Erasmus during the time of the ideological and political fury surrounding Charles's reign. Alfonso belonged to the inner circle of the Emperor Charles V, became the king's secretary in 1526, and died of the plague in 1532. Thus much of Ricapito's theory rests on the Parliament date of 1525. Ricapito goes on to study the similarity of style and critical tone between the novel and Alfonso's works, especially the first part of the *Diálogo de Mercurio y Carón* (*Dialogue of Mercury and Charon*). For him the first part of the *Dialogue* contains the same trickery, satire, and critical irony as the novel. Ricapito believes that the Squire comes closest to Valdesian thought. He also refers to Baltassare Castiglione's allusion to Alfonso's Jewish ancestry which Asensio approached with caution when he considered Américo Castro's theory that the author was a convert.[27] The reference is to Castiglione's scathing letter which was provoked by Alfonso's defense of the sacking of Rome. Of course this allusion to Alfonso's possible Jewish ancestry does not detract from Ricapito's hypothesis. Basically Ricapito's arguments rest on the comparison of literary style, and his conclusion that the author is Alfonso de Valdés or someone who belonged to the same intellectual circle is well argued and must be taken seriously.

The author, who undoubtedly wished to remain anonymous, has had his wish fulfilled. Not only does the author remain unknown today, but his narrator is obscured, and his point of view is so shrouded by irony that it is not obvious to readers and critics. Still, the only real evidence on which to base opinions is the text. The author is thought to be a convert by some, a New Christian, an aristocratic Old Christian, and an Erasmian by others. The primary source, the text, subtle and ironic as it is, makes the problem of identifying the author improbable if not impossible. From its inception the novel has drawn the attention of critics who search for the identity of the author, and to this date the problem has not been dismissed. People have refused to relegate to anonymity such a provocative, fine work.

In sum the author's sophisticated and inventive style which incorporates references to the classics, the Bible, folklore, proverbs, and literature shows him to be an eclectic, well-educated representative of the Renaissance. His narrative style, always ironic, sometimes satirical, and the skeptical tone of the work lead one to conclude that the author was a humanist and almost surely an Erasmian.

Chapter Five
Analysis of the Novel
Plot

Through an inventive use of first-person narrative, the unknown author, who hides behind his narrator, presents the prologue as having been written by the adult character Lázaro, a town crier of Toledo. The writing of the prologue and the novel is ostensibly an obedient act of the protagonist. It is addressed to a gentleman known only as "Your Grace," who is referred to in the last chapter as a friend of the Archpriest of San Salvador, Lázaro's final master and intimate of his wife.

The prologue states that the book which follows will speak of important events heretofore never heard nor seen. Those who read it carefully will derive pleasure from it. The narrator cites Pliny and Cicero in an act of mock erudition. He then confesses that he is no better than anyone else, and that his story is merely a trifle, written in a crude manner by a man who has endured much misfortune, danger, and disaster. Finally he addresses a gentleman known as "Your Grace" who wishes to know about Lázaro's "affair," that is his marital arrangement. In order for the gentleman to know all about him, Lázaro will start his story from the beginning and present it in great detail. The prologue ends with a particularly insightful sentence written in a sarcastic vein which explains the intention of the work. The narrator would like those who are proud of being high-born to realize how little this is worth, since Fortune smiled on them, and how much more worthy are those who by dint of effort and cunning have endured misfortune, rowed hard, and reached a good port.

"Well, first of all I want Your Grace to know that my name is Lázaro de Tormes (Lazarus of Tormes), son of Tomé González and Antona Pérez, who lived in Tejares, a village near Salamanca." Thus begins chapter 1. Lazarillo's surname comes from the peculiar circumstances of his birth. His father worked at a mill set on the River Tormes, and his mother, who was there one night, gave birth to him right on the river. He takes his name as a literary figure from

the fact that he was born on the River Tormes. When Lazarillo was
eight years old his father was convicted of stealing flour from
customers' sacks. After being soundly punished, the father joined
an expedition against the Moors and died in a battle on the coast of
North Africa. His mother, finding herself in dire straits, goes to the
city and takes a job cooking meals for students and washing clothes
for the stableboys of the Commander of Magdalena's estate. The
widow soon makes the acquaintance of Zaide, a black stable hand.
At first Lazarillo is afraid of Zaide, but he quickly learns that the
black man's visits mean food and firewood. One of the consequences of the visits is that Lazarillo acquires a dark-skinned half-
brother. The Commander's steward, who gets wind of the affair,
begins to miss oats and stable equipment and finds out that Zaide
has been stealing them. The poor stepfather is flogged, basted in
hot fat, and told not to see Lazarillo's mother again.

To avoid further scandal Lazarillo's mother becomes a servant at
an inn in a different neighborhood. A blind man who comes to the
inn one day asks to have Lazarillo as a guide. The mother agrees,
gives her son some advice on how to succeed in life, and sends him
on his way. The boy's education begins at this point. The Blind Man
(henceforth all of the characters are nameless) is shrewd, tightfisted,
and tough. As they leave the city they pass a stone statue of a bull.
The Blind Man tells the boy to put his ear close to the statue and
listen for a loud noise. The old man smashes Lazarillo's head against
the bull, hard enough for his ears to ring for three days. He laughs
and tells the boy that he, as a blind man's guide, has got to be
sharper than a needle. At this moment Lazarillo wakes from his innocence and realizes that he is alone in the world and has got to look
after himself. The Blind Man becomes Lazarillo's tutor in survival
and cunning. He keeps close tabs on his money, food, and wine.
The boy, who is hard put to survive and is suffering from hunger,
engages in a relentless battle of wits with the Blind Man in order to
obtain food, and receives some beatings for his efforts. For example,
one day they are squatting by the fire, and the Blind Man has his
hand over the mouth of his wine jug. Lazarillo has bored a tiny hole
in the jug, and sitting between the Blind Man's legs and lifting his
head, he lets the liquid trickle into his mouth. The suspicious Blind
Man, who has already found the hole as well as the wax which
Lazarillo melted to seal it, does not let on that he knows the boy's

scheme. When Lazarillo is in the position of receiving the wine, the Blind Man raises the jug and brings it down with great force on Lazarillo's face, breaking some of his teeth. From this time on Lazarillo dislikes the Blind Man. On another occasion he steals and eats a roasting sausage from a spit and substitutes a rotten turnip for it. When the Blind Man bites into his supposed sausage he rears up with rage, forces the boy's mouth open, and thrusts his nose into Lazarillo's throat to see if he has eaten it. Because of the Blind Man's long nose, and Lazarillo's fear, and because the sausage was barely chewed and digested, the boy throws up in the old man's face. Lazarillo is soundly beaten, his neck and throat scratched, his hair pulled out, and is barely saved by some neighbors who intervene. Resolved to leave his master, Lazarillo guides him to a stone pillar, leaps across a stream of water, hides behind the pillar, then tells the old man to jump. The old man gives a mighty leap, cracks his head on the pillar, and falls senseless to the ground. Lazarillo leaves, having taken his revenge, and taunts the Blind Man with the fact that he was able to smell the sausage but not the pillar. The first chapter ends with the young boy's having learned enough about cunning from his tutor to teach the teacher a lesson.

Lazarillo leaves his first master and joins a priest who is even more miserly than the Blind Man. The Priest himself lives and eats well mostly in other people's houses, but he starves the boy who is only allowed an onion every fourth day. Lazarillo once again has to use his wits to survive. He begins to steal bread from his master's chest which is always kept locked. Being an altar boy as well as a servant, Lazarillo eats well only when he attends funerals, and he actually prays for people to die in order that he may eat and survive. The boy remains with the Priest, who almost starves him to death, because he fears that other masters may be worse. Luckily Lazarillo meets a tinker who makes him a key to fit the chest, and the boy begins to enter his "breadly paradise" by filching the bread. The alarmed priest believes that rats have invaded the chest and nails up the holes in it securely. Lazarillo makes new holes and the puzzled priest concludes that a snake is stealing the bread. Lazarillo keeps the key in his mouth while he sleeps, and one night the key shifts so that the boy's breathing results in a whistling sound. The priest takes this to be the hissing of a snake, seizes a club, and in the dark, mistaking Lazarillo for a snake, knocks the boy out with a blow.

When the boy recovers from his wounds, the priest throws him out, declaring that Lazarillo is so wily that he must have been the servant of a blind man.

Hoping to find employment in a larger city and to further his fortunes, Lazarillo travels to Toledo. One day a squire asks Lazarillo, who is begging in the streets, to become his servant. The boy, thinking that he has found a wealthy master, since the Squire appears well-dressed, follows him home to a gloomy bare house. After waiting a long time for a meal, the boy is undeceived and realizes that the Squire has no food. He is a would-be gentleman who loathes manual labor and is concerned with keeping up aristocratic pretensions. Lazarillo now has to fend not only for himself but for the Squire as well. Again he begins to beg for bread. While eating his crusts on one occasion, the boy is surprised to see his master join him. Thus, as time passes, both of them live on what Lazarillo can beg. At last the Squire procures a bit of money and sends Lazarillo out for bread and wine. On the way the boy encounters a funeral procession and hears the widow lamenting that they are taking her husband to the gloomy house where there is neither food nor drink. Thinking that the procession is headed for the Squire's house, the innocent boy runs home and warns his master. The Squire leaves town at the end of the month without paying his rent, and Lazarillo is left to face the bailiffs and the wrathful creditors. After some difficulty he persuades the bailiffs of his innocence and is allowed to go free.

Chapter 4, full of innuendo, is very brief. It sketches Lazarillo's service with a friar of the Order of Mercy. The friar has women who refer to him as a relative, and he is interested in worldly affairs and social life. He gives Lazarillo his first pair of shoes which last the boy less than a week. Because of the running around he does and because of some other things which he would rather not mention, Lazarillo leaves his fourth master. In this chapter Lazarillo is more an observer than a protagonist.

His next master is a pardoner, a dealer in indulgences, and an accomplished rogue. Rumors begin to spread that the indulgences that he sells are false, and a constable comes to accuse the Pardoner publicly in church. The wily Pardoner prays to God for a miracle to punish his false accuser. Hardly does the Pardoner utter his prayer when the constable falls down in a fit foaming at the mouth. The Pardoner then prays for and forgives the constable. He puts an indulgence on his head, and little by little the constable recovers to the astonishment of the believers. Of course, the Pardoner sells many indulgences, and later, when the innocent Lazarillo sees the Pardoner and the constable laughing together, he realizes that the whole affair had been planned by the crafty Pardoner.

In the final chapter the boy has become a man. As Lázaro, he states that after having left the priest he went to work for a constable but did not stay long with him because the job was dangerous. Finally, Lázaro lands a civil service job as town crier, and he takes a cut from the sale of wine and all other business transactions that go through him. The Archpriest of San Salvador, a friend of the gentleman known as "Your Grace," notices how sharp-witted Lázaro is in announcing the sale of the priest's wines. He therefore arranges a marriage between Lázaro and a maid of his. The woman is publicly reputed to be the Archpriest's mistress and to have borne him three children. She and Lázaro receive frequent and substantial gifts. One day the Archpriest asks Lázaro if he has heard rumors about his wife. Lázaro replies that he has, whereupon he is advised sagely by the Archpriest to think of his profit rather than his honor, which is exactly what he does. Lázaro states that he has been silent about this marital arrangement until this point. "Your Grace" has become interested in the "affair" and has asked for an explanation of it. This has prompted Lázaro to write the account of his life. The book ends with a sarcastic sentence describing Lázaro—the town crier and a cuckold—at the height of prosperity and good fortune.

The novel offers a cynical antidote to the idealistic secular and religious world views of the Renaissance. The book deplores corruption and hypocrisy but does so without asking for reform, and although it focuses on the lower levels of society, it does so without malice.

Title

The book to be treated in this study has the following elements: a title, *La vida de Lazarillo de Tormes y de sus fortunas y adversidades* (The *Life of Lazarillo de Tormes and His Fortunes and Adversities*); a prologue; seven chapters called *tratados* ("tractates") written for the most part in the first person, each one containing an epigraph in the third person, which declares briefly the content of the chapters; and some supplementary paragraphs, certainly not written by the original author, which appeared in the Alcalá de Henares edition.

Lazarillo de Tormes is ironic from start to finish, from its very title to its final sentence. At first glance the twelve words of the title seem straightforward enough. They project the rhetorical solemnity which was reserved for biographies written about important people of the time. Other works written on famous people of the time had similar titles which often included the words "fortunes and adversities."[1] However, in the case of *Lazarillo de Tormes* the word *fortunas* ("fortunes") is ambiguous, for it really applies to the good and bad fortunes of the protagonist. Thus the words "fortunes and adversities" are both synonymous and antonymous. The name Lazarillo in the title does not symbolize an illustrious person but rather the opposite. For Spaniards of the Renaissance the name Lazarus carried with it the connotation of misery, poverty, and death, and the dimunitive further indicates the status of the central character. There are some scholars who believe that the word *laceria* ("misery," "poverty"), which appears various times in the novel, is phonically related to the diminutive Lazarillo.[2] The protagonist has also been linked to the biblical characters of that name, one being the man Jesus raised from the dead (John 11:1–44), and the other, a beggar (Luke 16:19–31). In both biblical narratives, Lazarus dies physically but is reborn into a spiritual life. Some critics view the life of Lazarillo de Tormes symbolically and believe that the protagonist dies spiritually and enters into a life of material well-being.[3] The title continues in its ironic vein with the name Tormes. Illustrious chivalric heroes took their names from their places of birth or from exotic places where extraordinary adventures occurred. In this case the River Tormes is an ordinary and accessible place, not at all marvelous or even exceptional, and the hero will later tell us in a humorous manner that he was born in a very unchivalric manner right on the river, hence his name, Lazarillo de Tormes.[4] The title, then, which is ironic in content and meaning, does not depict the life of an important person or an idealized knight, but rather that of an insignificant person, the son of Antona Pérez and Tomé González, who overcomes great adversities and misfortune only to "rise" to the dubious position of town crier and complacent cuckold.

Prologue

The narrative technique of the prologue and of the entire novel is of paramount importance because of the relationship that develops between author, protagonist, and reader. The prologue, like the title, is an instrument of irony and dissimulation and is intimately related in form and substance to the work as a whole. Only after reading the entire novel does one come to understand fully its content. The narrator of the prologue is not the frail innocent boy Lazarillo whose youth is described in the first three chapters, but rather the adult Lázaro who emerges in chapter 7 as a town crier, and it is he who speaks here. The cultured author, certainly not a lowly town crier, hides behind his character Lázaro, the adult protagonist/narrator, and allows him to reveal and/or withhold information as he sees fit. But it is only after finishing the novel that the reader realizes that Lázaro is a dubious character who controls the text. Because of his self-interest and his dissimulation, he presents himself in a positive manner and is not a reliable narrator of his life story.

Another thought-provoking aspect of the prologue is its duality. [5] Not only is it divided into two parts but it seems to be directed to two audiences. The second part clearly shows that it, as well as the book, is addressed to a gentleman known as "Your Grace," while the first part, which treats the universal themes of fame and honor, seems to be directed to a wide audience. The first sentence of the prologue continues the same ironic tone of the title and pompously promises material that will be of interest to many people: "I think it is good that important events, which by chance have never been seen nor heard, should come to the attention of many people and not be buried in the grave of oblivion." Yet the sentence, written in pseudoheroic style, is filled with deception and irony, for what follows is a story of a dishonorable man of low social and moral status, and the narrative is written in prosaic style at that.

Autobiographical literature of the Renaissance dealt with illustrious people and their famous deeds. This novel, on the other hand, mocks the lofty ideals of the Renaissance and is thoroughly ironic in its treatment of them. This sentence in the prologue identifies the narrator as a writer who surmises that some readers will find things in the book that please them and that those who read it very carefully will be delighted. The writer also tells us that there are at least two levels of understanding the work, and he suggests that there is something meaningful below its humorous surface.

Following the standard procedure of prologues written at this time, the author next establishes his erudition by including references to the classics. He starts by quoting Pliny: "there is no book however bad it may be, that does not have something good about it." Then, commenting on the diversity of readers' tastes, he says that everyone ought to have an opportunity to read his book since it is harmless enough and some benefit can be derived from it. Establishing himself as a writer, who is sensitive to his work, he asserts that writing a book is not easy and that few authors write for themselves alone. They go through the trouble of composing a book because they want to be rewarded, not so much financially as with approbation. The writer then quotes Cicero—"honor encourages the arts"—and states that it is the desire for praise that stimulates a soldier's bravery, a preacher's sermons, and an author's literary work. He explains that the soldier who is first to reach the top of the scaling ladder does so, not because he hates life, but because he wants praise. It is the desire to be extolled that makes him expose himself to danger. And so it is for arts and letters. The new doctor of theology who preaches well wants, of course, to save the immortal souls of his flock, but it does not displease him to be praised for his sermon. Then there is the nobody who jousts poorly but gives the banner bearing his arms to the poet who has praised the way he used his lance. What would he have done had the approbation been justified, the narrator asks.

At this point the prologue descends from the lofty topics of praise, honor, and glory to the lowly picaresque life which is contrasted with the heroism of the soldier, the preacher, and the writer. The tone changes to one of suspicious humility as the narrator states that he is no better than anyone else and refers to his story as a *nonada* ("trifle"): "I confess that I am not holier than my neighbors, and I write about this trifle in this crude style . . . and I think it is a good thing for readers to know that there is a living man who has endured so much misfortune, danger, and adversity."[6] False modesty was a device which was commonplace in prologues of this time. Here the writer does not promise a loftiness of character or of style, but he, like other authors, has a strong desire for readers to come to know his protagonist.

Up to the last paragraph of the prologue the author presents his material in a more or less objective manner and directs it to a general audience. But in the last paragraph the duality of the prologue and a change in discourse become apparent. At this point the prologue becomes a personal message addressed to a specific person known only as "Your Grace."

Y pues Vuestra Merced escribe se le escriba y relate el caso muy por extenso, parecióme no tomalle por el medio sino del principio porque se tenga entera noticia de mi persona, y también porque consideren los que heredaron nobles estados cuán poco se les debe, pues fortuna fue con ellos parcial, y cuánto más hicieron los que, siéndoles contraria con fuerza y maña remando salieron a buen puerto.[7]

Your Grace has written and asked me to write and tell you of the affair in detail, so I thought I would start at the beginning, not the middle, so that you would have a complete account of my life. I would also like those people who are proud of being high born to realize how little this means, since Fortune smiled on them, and how much more worthy are those who have suffered misfortune, but by dint of effort and cunning, have rowed and reached a good port.

It seems that "Your Grace" requested the author to write and describe in detail the *caso* ("affair"). This important sentence arouses the interest and curiosity of the reader who wants to know the identity of "Your Grace," why he has asked that an account be written, and what the "affair" really is. How will the protagonist overcome adverse fortune and succeed in reaching a "good port?" And most importantly, who is the narrator/protagonist who does all of this? By arousing the curiosity in such a manner, the author stimulates the reader to turn the page and begin reading the story which will answer these questions.

The narrator of the novel is Lázaro, the town crier, and in a supposed act of obedience, he is writing an account of the "affair" in the form of an epistle. The letter is addressed to "Your Grace" who surfaces in the final chapter as an acquaintance of the Archpriest of Saint Salvador, Lázaro's last master and confidant of his wife. No further identification of this noble individual is given, although he plays an important role in the structure of the narrative. It is he who ostensibly prompts the narrator to relate in the first person the story of his life and to tell it "from the beginning" in order that

"Your Grace" may know all about the protagonist. Thus, in the last paragraph of the prologue the narrator addresses a specific character of the novel in the first person, thereby becoming himself an entity of fiction. He is a narrator both by character (recounting his life at the request of "Your Grace"), and by narrative technique (a hidden author writing in the first person). At this point the narrator seems to have the distance and control necessary to relate his life story in detail without being too subjective. Of course this does not happen. The reader does not receive a "complete account" of his life, and ultimately the narrator emerges as a true *pícaro*, a devious social delinquent and rogue whose narration cannot be taken as absolute truth.

Lázaro, the narrator of the prologue, goes on to praise self-made men and diminish those who have inherited noble estates. The final sentence is ambiguous and has caused considerable perplexity among critics. The "good port" that Lázaro reaches is the "summit of good fortune" that he mentions in the last sentence of the book. Both expressions refer to his insignificant job and his ignoble *ménage à trois*, and the adjective "good" used here and throughout the book is laden with sarcasm.[8] In the pseudosuccess story which is about to follow the protagonist will attempt to improve his life by using "fuerza y maña" ("effort and cunning") as a means to an end. Lázaro follows the example of his mother who, "como sin marido y sin abrigo se viese, determinó arrimarse a los buenos por ser uno dellos . . ." ("finding herself without a husband or shelter, decided to mix with the good people so that she could become one of them . . ."). He progresses materialistically but suffers a series of disillusionments and failures, and in the end he is as insecure as he was in the beginning. His so-called success, the "good port" that he reaches, depends on the whims and lust of the Archpriest. It too falls under the rule of Fortune, and can disappear at any time.

Thus the author establishes a cyclical narrative that begins where it ends. It is the protagonist at the end of the story who narrates the story and the prologue, and it is he who states that he will give a "full account" of his life starting from the beginning. With the prologue the reader is skillfully prepared for the first chapter, since he is now curious as to the identity of the protagonist, his "affair," and his "good port." Of course it would be impossible for the narrator to give a full account of his life, and considering the brevity of the book, one does not expect great detail. What the author does is to allow Lázaro, his protagonist/narrator, to arrange the story to satisfy the curiosity of "Your Grace." Lázaro's point of view justifies the material he chooses to relate and omit. The series of events that are portrayed partially justify Lázaro's "affair." By the end of the novel the reader knows that what the narrator promised in the prologue, namely, the story of his entire life, is really not what has been written. In effect, Lázaro reveals mostly external actions which show him to be an overtly hypocritical social conformist. His innermost feelings, emotions, and moral judgments, for the most part, are concealed.

The brief prologue to *Lazarillo de Tormes* shows great literary skill. There is a reason for every word, every sentence. Its parodic material, its irony, its sarcastic tone, and its narrative technique relate it intrinsically to the novel.

Chapter 1

The first chapter is preceded by an epigraph, "Cuenta Lázaro su vida y cuyo hijo fue" ("Lázaro tells of his life and whose son he was"), which makes it appear as if the narrator, Lázaro the adult, will trace his biography like so many other books about heroes, starting with his noble genealogy and announcing the extraordinary circumstances of his birth and early childhood.[9] The narrator tells of his birth, his parents, his mother's widowhood, and his stepfather in a prosaic way, and all of this takes some twenty-one sentences. The bulk of the chapter deals with Lazarillo and his first master, the Blind Man.

The narrator begins chapter 1 telling "Your Grace" of his humble birth and parents, thereby establishing the parodic intention of the novel: "Well, first of all Your Grace should know that they call me Lázaro de Tormes, son of Tomé González and Antona Pérez, who lived in Tejares, a village near Salamanca. I was actually born right on the River Tormes, and that is how I took my surname. . . ." Lázaro's parents are the only characters in the book that have surnames, and they are the names of common folk. Even the protagonist's name is not given as Lázaro González Pérez; he is

known only as Lazarillo/Lázaro de Tormes. In a parody of the
chivalric romance, *Amadís de Gaula*, Lázaro gives a realistic mock-
heroic account of his birth. Amadís, a heroic knight, was floated
down a river at his birth, and Lazarillo claims to have been born on a
river. Lazarillo's father was in charge of a water mill on the Tormes,
and his pregnant mother was there one night. Her time came and
the child was born in the mill on the river.

Most critics believe that the name Lázaro was chosen for its
biblical connotations of Lazarus as a prototype of suffering. The
story of the protagonist does have some similarity to Lazarus the
beggar's story which is as follows:

There was a certain rich man, which was clothed in purple and fine linen,
and fared sumptuously every day: And there was a certain beggar named
Lazarus, which was laid at his gate, full of sores. And desiring to be fed
with the crumbs which fell from the rich man's table: moreover the dogs
came and licked his sores. And it came to pass, that the beggar died, and
was carried by the angels into Abraham's bosom: the rich man also died,
and was buried; And in hell he lifted up his eyes, being in torments, and
seeth Abraham afar off, and Lazarus in his bosom. (Luke 16:19-23)

Lazarillo is depicted as a miserable beggar, especially in chapters 1
and 3. Scholars have recently studied the connection between the
protagonist and the biblical version of the resurrected Lazarus and
believe that there are similarities between the two.[10] The story of the
resurrected Lazarus is described thus:

Now a certain man was sick, named Lazarus, of Bethany, the town of Mary
and her sister Martha. . . . Then when Jesus came, he found that he had
lain in the grave four days already. . . . Jesus therefore again groaning in
himself cometh to the grave. It was a cave, and a stone lay upon it. Jesus
said, "take ye away the stone. . . ." Then they took away the stone from
the place where the dead was laid. And Jesus lifted up his eyes, and said,
"Father, I thank thee that thou has heard me. And I knew that thou
hearest me always: but because of the people which stand by I said it, that
they may believe that thou has sent me." And when he thus had spoken,
he cried with a loud voice, "Lazarus, come forth." And he that was dead
came forth, bound hand and foot with graveclothes: and his face was
bound about with a napkin. Jesus saith unto them, "Loose him, and let
him go." (John 11:17, 38-39, 41-44)

When one studies the theme of death in the novel carefully, the
relationship between the protagonist and the John 11 version is

strengthened. For sixteenth-century readers the name Lazarus was rich in evocative power, and it probably carried with it a connotation combining the two biblical versions. [11] This combination comes to mind when one sees the child protagonist who begs, and his cycles of near-death and rebirth.

Viewed in this light, the first two sentences of the novel introduce not a hero of noble lineage but a humble protagonist who will suffer, have some brushes with death, and in some way be reborn. Besides the pseudoheroic language in the beginning of the chapter, there are some daring parodies of the Bible. Describing how his father had stolen and been taken prisoner, the narrator parodies John 1:20: "he confessed and did not deny anything and suffered persecution under the law." [12] Continuing, he says bitterly of his father: "I hope to God that he is in Heaven, because the Gospel calls people like him blessed," which is a sardonic parody of Matthew 5:10. [13]

The first misfortune to befall Lazarillo is the death of his father in an expedition against the Moors, at Los Gelves and his widowed mother, finding herself in dire straits, "determinó arrimarse a los buenos por ser uno dellos . . ." ("decided to associate with the good people in order to become one of them . . ."). Who are the "good" people in the novel? The ironical use of the word *bueno* (good) causes a reversal of the normal ethical values held in Christian Spain at this time. That which is good is sure; it gives the protagonist what he needs to combat adverse Fortune. [14] Later in the novel, in chapter 7, when the Archpriest tells Lázaro not to pay attention to rumors connecting the priest with his wife and to think only about what profits him, the protagonist, following his mother's example, answers, "Señor . . . yo determiné de arrimarme a los buenos . . ." ("Sir . . . I decided to associate with the good people . . ."). In almost the exact words used to describe his mother's actions, Lázaro shows that he has become one of the "good" people that he describes throughout the book. [15] In chapter 1, however, it is necessity that drives his mother to do what she does, whereas he consciously chooses to do what he does.

In order to avoid danger, Lazarillo's mother goes to the city and tries to earn a living by mixing with the "good" people. Among other jobs she washes clothes for stablehands of the Commander de la Magdalena, and befriends a black man called Zaide. The narrator says euphemistically that his mother and Zaide came to "know" one another. Zaide comes to the house and leaves in the morning.

He provides Lazarillo and his mother with necessities like food and firewood by stealing from the Commander. Antona's contractual arrangement with Zaide, which implies mutual profit and sex for necessities, provides the boy with a stepfather and material security. Continuing the "stay and the conversation," Lazarillo's mother gives him a little black baby brother. The narrator describes the black stepfather playing one day with his stepbrother who, seeing that Lazarillo and his mother are white and that his father is not, becomes frightened and runs from the black man calling him a bogeyman. This incident, disguised as serious narrative, includes one of the thirteen asides addressed to the reader:[16] "Although I was only a boy, I thought a lot about what my little brother had said and asked myself: 'How many people must there be in a world who run away from others in fright because they do not see themselves?'" With the asides, the narrator forges a special relationship between protagonist and reader and thus later can elicit sympathy for Lázaro's cause. The narrator had already promised in the prologue that those who read the book carefully will be delighted, and the asides are meant for these careful readers. In the asides the *histor* not only recounts but observes and gives the reader an opportunity to pause and reflect on the action.

With Zaide's presence in the household, life improves for Lazarillo and his mother Antona, but adverse fortune, which had taken Lazarillo's father at Los Gelves, strikes again, and Zaide too suffers at the hands of justice. He, like Lazarillo's father, steals in order to provide the necessities for life. Zaide is caught, whipped, and basted with hot oil for stealing and for having an illicit relationship with Lazarillo's mother, who, in turn, is threatened with punishment if she is seen with Zaide again. Thus Antona, in order to avoid rumors and danger, leaves the neighborhood and takes a job as servant at an inn. There she meets a blind man who asks the widow if he may have Lazarillo as a guide, promising to treat the boy like a son. In a brief farewell scene Antona gives Lazarillo to the man and tearfully says good-bye to the boy, giving him her benediction and some advice: "I know I'll never see you again. Try to be good and may God guide you. I have raised you and have placed you with a good master. Look after yourself." With this brief good-bye, the author terminates the first part of the chapter dealing with Lazarillo's prehistory, and portraying hardship, poverty, and society in a negative way. At this point Lazarillo leaves the world of family protection and love and enters into a new one filled with more danger and adversity than he has seen thus far.

The prehistory which describes Lazarillo's birth and family life with irony, euphemism, and parody sets up his initial situation, that of a young isolated orphan and an innocent victim of circumstance. In this way, the author establishes the possibility of the protagonist's breaking all ties of family and native city and gives him the opportunity to wander from place to place. With the sophisticated use of first-person narrative, the author elicits sympathy in favor of the innocent victim. This relationship is further strengthened by the protagonist's sharing his actions and some private observations and thoughts in the asides which are heard only by "Your Grace" and the reader.

The first part of the chapter ends with the separation of the boy from his mother, and the second begins when the Blind Man and Lazarillo leave Salamanca. This is the boy's initiation into society at large. The Blind Man, his teacher, will instruct the boy on how to get on in the world by using wit and cunning. There are distinct episodes in this chapter that coincide with different levels of Lazarillo's education. The first lesson comes when the Blind Man smashes Lazarillo's head against the stone bull. With this first lesson the Blind Man teaches Lazarillo that the world is filled with illusions and that the boy must learn to discern between appearances and reality. The blow to Lazarillo's head takes away the illusion that he has been placed with a "good master," and he realizes that he had better take care of himself. Sharing his thoughts with the reader, he says to himself: "What he says is true. I had better keep my eyes open because I am alone and I have got to look after myself." The aside emphasizes the boy's solitude. From the moment he says, "I am alone," he is one person who must survive by his wits against a hostile world.

Throughout this chapter there is a continuous string of tricks, illusions, and lies between master and guide, which show that things are not what they seem to be and that rarely do people speak the truth openly. As his teacher, the Blind Man says that he will not make Lazarillo a rich man but that he will show him how to make a living, and so the boy begins to use his intelligence to look after himself. The Blind Man is Lazarillo's substitute parent, but above all he is a master teacher on the art of survival. Commenting on the Blind Man's dexterity as a tutor, Lazarillo says, "después de Dios,

éste me dió la vida y siendo ciego, me alumbró y adestró en la carrera
de vivir" ("after God, he gave me life, and although he was blind,
he enlightened me and taught me what life was about"). Guillén
believes that the entire chapter is based on the initial wordplay on
the verb *adestrar,* which means to guide and to teach.[17] Actually
both characters change roles; at times they guide, and at times they
teach. Lazarillo describes the Blind Man as astute, cunning, and
sharp as a needle in his trade. This master knows hundreds of
prayers by heart and recites them for money. He earns more in one
month than a hundred blind men do in a whole year, because he
has endless ways of getting money out of people.

There is, nevertheless, a duality in the relationship between
teacher and student. Although the Blind Man teaches Lazarillo how
to survive, he is so miserly that he nearly starves the boy to death.
The theme of hunger is central in this chapter; it serves to motivate
the battle of wits which will ultimately take place. Since his master
does not give him half of what he needs to survive, Lazarillo uses
cunning and tricks to "bleed the avaricious sack" in which the
Blind Man hoards his food. He also steals wine from the "sweet and
bitter" jar that the Blind Man guards. Lazarillo learns the hard way
that the Blind Man's senses are quite sharp. When Lazarillo is sitting in front of a fire, between his master's legs, head up, catching
the wine trickling from the jar, the Blind Man, aware of the boy's
ruse, takes revenge:

with all his strength he lifted the jar, which had been the source of
pleasure and was now to be the instrument of pain, and from high over his
head he let it fall straight on my mouth, he let it fall with all the strength
he could muster. Poor Lázaro was not expecting this; in fact he was relaxed
and enjoying himself as before. I really felt as if the roof and everything on
it had fallen on top of me. The Blind Man's love tap was so hard that I was
knocked out and had bits of broken jar stuck in my face and was cut all
over. Some of my teeth were broken and that is why I have not got them in
my head till this day.

At this point the narrator retains enough distance to describe the
episode without bitterness. Indeed, he is so detached that he even
refers to himself in the third person, saying of the blow, "Poor
Lázaro was not expecting this . . . ." But the situation changes
instantaneously and dramatically. At the moment of impact the

narrative distance disappears, and the narrator continues in the first person.

This scene, like others in this chapter, contains a battle of wits which ends in physical violence and its consequences. Lazarillo has learned a lesson, but in the process he has lost some teeth which he lacks "till this day." His view of his master changes, and his desire for vengeance begins here. The protagonist shares his observations and thoughts with the reader as he says: "From that time on I disliked the cruel Blind Man, and although he treated me kindly by bandaging up my cuts, I could easily see that he had enjoyed his sadistic punishment." The boy begins to think that "a few more love taps like that one from the cruel Blind Man would get rid of me, so I decided to get rid of him first. But I did not do it right away since I wanted to be sure that I would come out of it all right." Lazarillo seethes with anger, and his plans for revenge are calculated.

The punishment continues as the Blind Man begins to kick and hit the boy for no reason at all. Yet the Blind Man is not portrayed simply as a cruel man. His cruelty is tempered by his sense of humor and wisdom. In spite of Lazarillo's suffering, he continues to respect the Blind Man as a teacher, and he, as well as we, appreciate the old man's sense of humor and his ability to tell a story. When the Blind Man later recounts the episode of the wine jar to passersby, they laugh at his manner of telling the story and at the boy's devilish ingenuity. Lazarillo's vengeance comes in stages; it starts slowly as he begins to lead his master deliberately along rocky and muddy roads in order to make his feet sore and cause him to trip.

Lazarillo's next lesson demonstrates the Blind Man's wisdom that he has come to respect. They arrive at Almorox when the grapes are being harvested, and a picker gives them a very ripe bunch out of charity. The Blind Man, knowing that if he stores them in the sack they will turn to liquid, makes an agreement with Lazarillo. In order for both to get their fair share they agree to eat one grape at a time. But neither of them honors the contract. The sagacious Blind Man tells Lazarillo that he knows that he has been cheated: "¿Sabes en qué veo que las comiste tres a tres? En que comía yo dos a dos y callabas"[18] ("Do you know how I saw that you were eating three grapes at a time? Because I was eating two at a time and you did not say anything"). Lazarillo laughs to himself and marvels at the old man's wisdom. The Blind Man has demonstrated that one need not have eyes to understand human behavior. But by demonstrating the wisdom of the teacher in this fashion the author also emphasizes the wit of the student who will later surpass his master.

The next episode deals with the turnip and is narrated in a graphic naturalistic manner, eliciting humor and revulsion at the same time. Its crudeness is diminished by Lazarillo's cunning and the humorous description of the Blind Man. The war between teacher and student reaches its culmination here. The preliminary scene is set when the Blind Man gives Lazarillo a sausage to roast, then gives him some money and sends him for wine. Sharing his thoughts with the reader Lazarillo claims the Devil put temptation before his eyes, and exchanges a rotten turnip for the sausage which he wolfs down. The following scene which portrays the Blind Man searching for the stolen sausage is repulsive but humorous. Similar scenes will later appear in *Guzmán de Alfarache,* the *Buscón,* and *Don Quixote.* The Blind Man seizes Lazarillo's head, forces his mouth open, and, following the scent like a bloodhound, thrusts his long nose down the boy's throat. Given the terror that Lazarillo experiences, the brief time that the sausage had to settle in his stomach, and the length of the Blind Man's sharp nose, the boy chokes, and, as the narrator says: ''the deed and my greed were revealed and the stolen property was returned to its rightful owner . . . before he could get his trunk out of my mouth, my stomach was so upset that I threw up, and his nose and the half-digested sausage left my mouth at the same time.'' The reader has previously observed the Blind Man's anger and cruelty and can well imagine what the poor boy's punishment will be for this deed. Lazarillo expects a bad time and exclaims, ''Oh Great God, I wish I had been in my grave at that moment because I was as good as dead.'' The boy is beaten so severely that if it were not for the intervention of other people, the narrator says that the Blind Man would have killed him. Later, when the Blind Man recounts the episode, he shows his skill in telling a story. His tale is so amusing that even Lazarillo has to laugh at it. The old man includes in his story the episodes of the jar of wine, the grapes, and the sausage, and the narrator says: ''People laughed so loud that even passersby came in to share in the festivities. The Blind Man told of my deeds in such a funny manner that although I was bruised and crying, it appeared to me that it would not be fair if I myself did not laugh.'' Not only does the narrator share his physical misfortune and his anguish with the reader, but he goes one step further and has Lazarillo laugh at his own expense, thereby eliciting even more sympathy for him. Frank Durand observes the author's sophisticated interest in narrative skill and comments on the Blind Man's extraordinary talent in telling an anecdote:

> The interest in narrative skill is of a very sophisticated kind: an author obviously proud of his narrative ability creates a first-person narrator who, in turn, not only reveals his enjoyment of his own choice of words and timing, but also admires his master's ability to relate adventures. The first-person narrator thus assumes the role of audience at a telling of his own story: the younger Lazarillo enjoys listening, even if the anecdote is at his own expense. By having Lazarillo comment on the "gracia y donayre" of the Blind Man, isn't the author, in fact, directing our attention to his own skill?[19]

After his beatings, some neighbors nurse Lazarillo back to health by washing his wounds with wine. The Blind Man comments that the boy ought to be more grateful for the wine than to his father, because the latter only begot the boy once, but wine has given him life a thousand times over. Then he is cast in the role of a prophet as he says to Lazarillo; "I tell you . . . that if anyone is going to be lucky with wine it will be you." The protagonist/narrator, who will sell wines in chapter 7, declares that "the Blind Man's prognostication proved right, and I have often thought of him since then . . . he must have had the gift of prophecy, and I am sorry for what I did to him. What he told me that day turned out to be absolutely true as Your Grace will hear in the future." The narrator here is an adult who is looking back on his past with the Blind Man and anticipating his position as a seller of wines in the last chapter.

The final episode, that of the pillar, is one of vengeance and justice. It marks the end of Lázaro's apprenticeship. The final lesson ends as the first one began—with someone's head being smashed against stone, but this time it is the Blind Man who receives a lesson from his student. Lazarillo and his master have been out begging, and because of a heavy rain the Blind Man suggests that they return to the inn. To do so they have to cross a stream of water which runs in the street. Lazarillo tells his master that he will guide him to a place where the stream is narrow so that they can jump across without getting their feet wet. Instead, Lazarillo leads him to a pillar. The boy jumps first, hides behind the pillar, and then tells his master to jump as hard as he can. Lazarillo comments: "At that moment God blinded his intellect in order to give me vengeance . . .," and the old man rears up like a billy goat, and jumps, crashing head first into the pillar and falling back half dead. Lazarillo recalls the episode of the turnip and jeers: "What? You smelled the sausage but not the pillar?" The boy has learned so well that he teaches the master a lesson in trickery.

Although this chapter borrows diverse anecdotes from folklore, it has unity in form and meaning. Apart from the introductory material in chapter 1 the series of episodes revolves around the two central figures and their battle of wits. The incidents are arranged in gradation, leading to a climax; their unifying element is the motivation of hunger, and their purpose is to teach. The episodes which revolve around inanimate objects (the bull, the sack, the jar of wine, the grapes, the turnip, and the pillar) have some elements of humor and are related to Lazarillo's education. The humor as well as the education stem from hunger, violence, and cunning, and Lazarillo, as a student of "fuerza y maña" ("effort and cunning"), learns his lessons well, teaches the teacher a trick or two, and graduates, as it were, *cum laude*.

Chapter 2

The second epigraph, "How Lázaro was placed with a cleric and what happened to him while in his service," is more accurate than that of the first chapter. Although most of the material in this chapter deals with the Priest of the Maqueda and Lazarillo, the overriding theme of hunger as the motivating force is present throughout. There is a progressive and climactic treatment of the hunger theme in the first three chapters.[20] The second chapter serves as a link between the other two. The connection is obvious from the very beginning of the chapter when the narrator reports that Lazarillo leaves the Blind Man, not knowing whether he is alive or dead, and comes to the town called Maqueda where a priest takes him as a servant. The boy is begging and approaches the Priest who asks him if he knows how to serve at mass. The Blind Man had taught Lazarillo how to serve, so he has the qualifications to be the

Priest's servant. In the fourth sentence of the chapter the reader sees the second stage of the hunger theme and how it relates to the first chapter. Lazarillo says of his new master: "I escaped from the frying pan and wound up in the fire; compared to this man the Blind Man was as generous as Alexander the Great." The tone is set immediately for Lazarillo's desperate fight for survival.

A description of the avarice and hypocrisy of the Priest follows. Once again Lazarillo is disillusioned. What appeared to be a religious man who would embody charity and piety turns out to be a miserable, hypocritical miser who almost starves the boy to death. Whereas the Blind Man was cruel but had his good points, this man has no redeeming qualities. The blatant anticlericalism of the chapter derives from the characterization of the Priest, which is so pointed that he almost comes off as a caricature. The narrator begins by treating the traditional sin of the clergy, avarice. He describes the Priest by saying that all the money-grabbing meanness of the world was embodied in this man: "I do not know if it was his nature or whether he assumed it when he took the habit." With this sentence the narrator begins his description of the Priest and establishes his anticlericalism at the same time. Bataillon states that the author's treatment of anticlericalism adds nothing to the medieval tradition, while Asensio argues that the criticism of the priestly and monastic life is a reflection of the Illuminist movement of the time.[21] Valbuena considers that this chapter has an Erasmian tone, which was in vogue in this era, and Ricapito sees in it clear strains of Erasmian thought.[22] Certainly the author's anticlericalism, for the most part, was simply a continuation of a medieval tradition. This does not make him an Erasmian, nor does it exclude him from that group. The medieval tradition of anticlericalism, its proverbs, and its language were all part of the patrimony of Spain, free to be used by the writers of the Renaissance, Erasmians or not.

In the novel the clergy plays a large part in a corrupt society for, as Del Monte says, Lázaro lives almost all of his life under the protection of the Church.[23] Deyermond points out correctly that the fact that the clergy is portrayed as evil need not imply hostility to Christianity or to the Catholic church. The Church occupied a central role in Spanish society at the time the novel was written, and it is a vital part of the book. Five of Lazarillo's nine masters are connected with religion in one way or another, and all of them have a profound influence on his life. The narrator's descriptions of these characters imply corruption and self-interest. The norm was set in the first chapter when the narrator speaks of Zaide's thievery, and says: "Why should we be surprised at priests when they steal from the poor or at monks when they rob things from the monasteries to give to their lady devotees, or others, when we see how love can make a poor slave do what he did." From the author's viewpoint the clergy and those who have dealings with the Church are representatives of society as a whole.

The Priest of the Maqueda has "poca caridad" ("little charity"), the Monk of the Order of Mercy is interested in "negocios seglares" ("secular matters"), and the Pardoner is the most shameless man the narrator has ever seen. The Chaplain mentioned in the sixth chapter is interested in business, and the Archpriest of the seventh is an adulterer. The author of the novel does not separate the Church from society nor does he condemn it or ask for reform. What he does is present it as a corrupt institution, part of a corrupt society seen through the eyes of a corrupt narrator/protagonist. He leaves the reader free to judge the clergy and its institution. The book's criticism of the avarice and sexual immorality of the clergy and the chicanery of the Pardoner is part of the medieval tradition, but the author goes beyond this point. He seems to prefer a personal devotion as opposed to outward ritual, and Lázaro's relationship with God is a special and private one.

Although the avaricious priest is common in medieval literature, no source has been found for the author's special treatment of the Priest of the Maqueda. This chapter may lack the variety of the first one, and it may not have the complex personal relationship between master and servant that the third chapter has, but, according to Lázaro Carreter, it contains the greatest inventiveness in the book. The system of articulating distinct episodes and the portrayal of Lazarillo as wandering itinerant servant is replaced here by a single episode and by Lazarillo, a domestic servant, confined within four walls, facing his antagonist, the chest. Such a limitation of possibilities carries with it a creative process that Lázaro Carreter calls a tour de force.[24]

The war against hunger takes place within the confines of the Priest's house which proves to be a dangerous environment for Lazarillo. The boy does battle with the securely locked chest in which the Priest hoards his food. Deyermond does not find it surprising that over two thirds of the images from warfare, chivalry,

and hunting occur in this chapter.[25] Whereas the Blind Man shared
from time to time some food with Lazarillo and taught the boy how
to survive, the Priest does not have these redeeming qualities. He
starves the boy, and if Lazarillo does not use his wits and do battle
with the chest, he will die of hunger. The Priest has a string of
onions and they are under lock and key. Lazarillo's ration is one
onion every four days, and the Priest gives the key to his servant with
these instructions: "here take it and bring it back right away, and
do not indulge your greed too much." With this sentence the Priest
combines his avarice with hypocrisy which proves to be as strong a
negative quality as the first. The Priest buys a dinner and eats meat
every evening. All Lazarillo gets is a piece of bread and gravy. On
Saturdays the Priest eats a sheep's head, as is the custom in the area,
and gives Lazarillo the bones that he has been gnawing on, saying:
"Take, eat, and triumph, for you it is the world. You live better
than the Pope himself." When Lazarillo hears this statement he
comments to himself, in the first aside of the chapter: "May God
give you a life like mine one day." Most of the asides in this chapter
are sarcastic in tone. With this one Lazarillo looks to God to be his
ally in vengeance. After three weeks of living from hand-to-mouth
with the Priest, Lazarillo is so weak from hunger that he cannot
stand on his feet. He describes his brush with death: "I saw quite
clearly that unless God and my wits remedied the situation, I was
heading for my grave." At this point he reminisces about the tricks
he played on the astute Blind Man, but the Blind Man lacked sight,
and this master, as the narrator mockingly observes, sees everything
and notices every coin going into the collection basket. "He kept
one eye on the people and the other on my hands, and his eyes
danced in his head as if they were balls of mercury."

The theme of hunger intensifies as the narrator describes the
priest's duties and presents his own thoughts and observations.
When Lazarillo and the Priest offer prayers at brotherhood meetings or at the homes of mourning, the Priest, the narrator reports,
eats like a wolf[26] as long as it is at someone else's expense. Funeral
feasts are the only occasions when Lazarillo is able to stuff himself
with food, and this leads him to pray to God that someone will die
every day. When he and his master go to the home of sick people to
administer extreme unction, the Priest asks those present to pray,
and Lazarillo prays for the sick person to die. He heaps blessings on
those who die, but, as he says: "If a sick person got better (God

forgive me), I cursed him over and over again. . . ." Lazarillo never
hates the human race but in order to eat he "prayed for God to kill
someone every day." His statement is an example of the black
humor in the novel, and with it the author begins to build an intimate and strong bond between Lazarillo and God.

The first references to God in the novel are in simple conventional language, for example, "my father, may God pardon him,"
but as early as chapter 1 God becomes Lazarillo's ally and brings
him the means of survival and vengeance, as He "blinds" the Blind
Man's intellect to allow Lazarillo revenge. One day when the
miserable Priest returns home, God grants that he not see the bread
that the "angel" has taken, and in the final chapter, God
"enlightens" the protagonist and puts him on a profitable course.
The intimate relationship between Lazarillo and God is further
heightened by the fact that Lazarillo shares his intimate observations, questions, and despair with no one but God and the reader.

In this chapter Lazarillo's praying for someone to die in order to
eat sets the tone of despair. He emphasizes the hopelessness of his
situation by lamenting that he sees no escape from his suffering except in death which he himself asks for: "So there was no relief in
death, which I wanted sometimes for myself as well as others. But it
never came, although it was always with me." The nearness of
death which Lazarillo reminds us of at various times in this chapter,
brings the hunger motif of the first chapter to its second level, and it
prepares the reader for the do-or-die battle that Lazarillo will have
with the chest. Lazarillo will either enter the chest and eat life-
sustaining food or die of starvation. Repeating a motif of the first
chapter, the author has him use all the cunning and inventiveness
he has in his fight for life. The narrator first sets the scene and the
situation by telling the reader that there is no escape, as Lazarillo
says: "I often thought of leaving my miserable master, but I did not
for two reasons. First, I did not trust my legs because they were so
weak from hunger. Second, I thought it through and said to myself,
'I've had two masters. The first kept me half-dead from hunger,
then I bump into this one who has me in my grave with it. If I leave
this one and find another who is worse, I'll perish for sure.'" The
author puts innocent thoughts of this type in the mind of his naive
protagonist, which sets a tone of despair, creates a type of black
humor, and builds upon the sympathy of the reader. He also
prepares the reader for the next chapter where the hunger theme

will reach its climax and where the reader will meet the Squire, Lazarillo's next master, who, in his way, is worse than this one. Up to this point in the chapter, the author dwells on the theme of hunger and describes Lazarillo's confining and dangerous situation from which it seems there is no escape. Now the story turns to the battle with the chest, a struggle which occupies most of the pages in the chapter. Not only does the focal point of the story change but the author's language becomes more ironic as he begins to make use of daring parodic metaphors on religion.

The religious metaphors and symbolism of this chapter have attracted the interest of several noted scholars, and their interpretations are for the most part insightful.[27] In chapter 2 the author uses religious metaphors in a bold way. He refers to the chest as a "breadly paradise"; Lazarillo, "enlightened by the Holy Spirit," arranges a plan whereby he gets aid from an "angelic" tinker who is "sent by God" to help the boy get into the chest;[28] once in it, Lazarillo sees the bread as the "face of God"; he pays the tinker with a piece of bread that he refers to as *bodigo* (a bread offering to the Church); the Priest appears and does not notice that one of the *obladas* (a bread offering for the dead) is missing; Lazarillo "adores" the bread not daring to "receive" it; and, finally, he refers to himself as a "serpent": the "serpent" that entered and was expelled from the "breadly paradise" by a representative of the Church. Guillén agrees with Castro that these metaphors very probably reveal the independent spirit of a New Christian of Jewish or Moslem descent.[29] Some critics view them as hererodoxical, and others see in them an Erasmian influence.[30]

Lazarillo is suffering his routine hunger when one day a tinker, "an angel sent by God," comes to the door to ask if there is anything for him to mend. In a sarcastic aside Lazarillo says to himself, "There is plenty to mend in me and you would have your work cut out for you if you were to repair me." This statement, which recalls the poor physical shape that the boy is in, is reserved only for "Your Grace" and the reader. At this point an idea of how to enter the chest comes to him, and, "enlightened by the Holy Spirit,"[31] he tells the tinker that he has lost the key to the chest and asks him to make a new one. The tinker makes a key, Lazarillo sees the "face of God,"[32] and pays the tinker with one of the *bodigos*. It is a compassionate God who has sent help to alleviate Lazarillo's suffering, but ironically, it is a God who has had to intervene and bypass the Priest, a minister of the Church. When the Priest leaves the house Lazarillo opens his "breadly paradise," takes one of the *bodigos,* and dispatches it in the time it takes to say "two credos." Later when Lazarillo sees the Priest looking at the loaves, counting and recounting them, he solicits help from Saint John, patron saint of servants. Feigning innocence, he prays secretly: "Saint John strike him blind." The Priest calculates the number of loaves that have been eaten and those that are remaining and begins to suspect foul play. This time when he leaves, Lazarillo, in an obvious reference to the Eucharist, consoles himself by opening the chest and beginning to "adore" the bread, not daring to "receive" it. The next few days Lazarillo can do nothing other than open the chest and look at the "face of God." Once again a compassionate God intervenes as a source of inspiration for Lazarillo. "God Himself who aids the afflicted" sees the boy in dire straits and brings to his mind a little trick. Lazarillo will take crumbs from the chest that is filled with holes, and his master will suspect the culprits to be mice. This comes to pass, and the Priest later offers Lazarillo a piece of bread which he thinks has been gnawed by mice, saying, "Eat this, a mouse is a clean animal."[33] The Priest thus combines his trait of miserliness with hypocrisy. He then takes measures to protect his property by covering the holes with boards and nails. When Lazarillo sees this he sinks to the depths of despair, and in his first long emotional outburst to God, he cries: "Oh my God . . . how much misery, misfortune, and disaster befall us who have been born, and how short-lived are the pleasures in our wretched lives." Such outbursts to God show another aspect of Lazarillo's thinking and his relationship with God. There are times when he does not understand God's plan or sense of justice, and there are instances when he loses hope and wants to put an end to his suffering. In moments of great anguish, he turns to God for relief or for an explanation. His total isolation is underlined by these appeals. To whom, other than God, can he turn?

All seems lost to Lazarillo when he sees the chest boarded up. However, he responds to his adversary by changing the culprit that the Priest will blame to a snake. Lazarillo pushes a knife through the chest like an auger making a small hole in it. The next day when the Priest notices the hole and some bread missing, he again boards up the chest. Lazarillo promptly makes another hole and reenters. With a reference to the *Odyssey,* he declares that he and the Priest "seemed to be following the same plan as Penelope and her weaving, because whatever he wove by day I undid at night." Neighbors remind the Priest that there used to be a snake in his house, and this must be the cause of the damage to the chest. From then on the Priest does not sleep soundly, listening for the snake. Lazarillo, who refers to himself as a "serpent," hides the "key" to his "breadly paradise" in his mouth at night when he sleeps. This proves to be his undoing. The narrator tells the reader in detail what happened:

one night when I was asleep, my mouth fell open and the key began to whistle as my breath passed over its hollow part . . . and my master heard it and believed without a doubt that it was the hissing of a snake; certainly it must have sounded that way to him. He got up very quietly with his club in his hand and following the sound of the snake . . . he thought that the snake was in the straw warming itself in the warmth of my body. Lifting the club high, thinking that the snake was beneath it and he would be able to kill it with one blow, he delivered such a blow to my head that he knocked me out and left me bleeding.

As Francisco Rico has observed, this passage shows the superb and subtle skill that the author has in narrating a realistic account of what happens to the protagonist.[34] Who is doing the narrating at this point? Lazarillo is asleep and cannot be an eyewitness narrator, but this can easily go undetected, because for almost all of the novel the narrator has been a *histor* telling the reader what he has observed. Here, he is sleeping, but the reader gets a graphic realistic description of the priest's stealthy approach, the noise of the key, and the blow that knocks Lazarillo unconscious. The author uses great skill in presenting the action as a well-founded supposition. He separates the real from the doubtful by the degree of probability conveyed in a verb: "certainly it *must have* sounded that way . . ." (my italics). Continuing his subtle manipulation of fact and hypothesis, the narrator says with reference to the Priest:

the cruel hunter must have said to himself: "I have found the mouse and the snake that have given me trouble and eaten my property." I cannot say for sure what happened during the next three days because I spent them in the belly of the whale.[35] But what I have just recounted I heard my master say when I came to. He told it often and at length to anybody who cared to listen.

After separating narrator and protagonist, the author makes the narrator a receiver of secondhand information. The realistic account is told as if Lazarillo has seen it, but it is, in fact, a matter of hearsay, and his confession that what he is recounting is based on what his master said ironically makes the narrator more credible. He can be trusted to distinguish between what he observes as *histor* and what he portrays himself.

After Lazarillo is cured, the Priest throws the boy out, saying that he is so crafty that he must have been a blind man's servant. Then crossing himself as if Lazarillo were the Devil himself, he goes into his house and slams the door shut.

In this chapter the author has shown himself to be a master of his trade by his inventiveness and his skillful use of language and metaphors. Always keeping the interest of the reader, he adroitly develops two characters locked within the confines of four walls and sets up a situation which clearly shows their personality traits. With his daring use of religious metaphors he gives life to inanimate objects and hints at his socio-religious views. Finally, with extraordinary dexterity, he distinguishes between *histor* and narrator creating a sense of *a posteriori* realism.

Chapter 3

In chapter 2 the protagonist apparently has reached the maximum degradation produced by misery and hunger; he goes "from the frying pan to the fire" and is afraid of leaving the Priest for fear of finding a master who is worse, for this would mean certain death. The third chapter completes a trilogy based on the theme of hunger which motivates most of the actions of Lazarillo and his first three masters.[36] The author has planned the action and themes of this trilogy very carefully. At the end of chapter 2 the Priest throws Lazarillo out, and that seems to be the end of an episode which carries with it misery and the threat of death. In chapter 3 the author continues with the theme of hunger and sets the scene immediately by having Lazarillo beg. The boy goes to the town of Toledo,[37] begins his traditional occupation, and is having a tough time of it. People chide him for begging, calling him a scoundrel and a loafer, and they tell him to find a master and get some work. Lazarillo, in the first aside of the chapter, wonders whether God has created a person he can work for. Here he is in Toledo begging at every door and having most of them slammed in his face, because "charity had disappeared in the heavens." He is struggling diligently when he chances to meet a squire.[38] The narrator describes the Squire as well dressed, neatly groomed, and apparently well off. The Squire approaches Lazarillo and asks if he is looking for work. The answer is yes, and the Squire responds, glorifying himself: "come along with me . . . God has blessed you having you bump into me. You must have prayed well today." At this point in the narrative Lazarillo, as well as some of the readers, is relieved; his suffering seems to have ended. Judging by the Squire's clothes and his bearing, he is the type of master that the boy needs. Lazarillo's hopes are high for the future. There follows a fairly detailed description of the city as the two walk to the master's house. The author's perspective has changed. Lázaro, as the narrator/protagonist, has become involved in the world around him and has begun to describe it to the reader.

Time in this chapter slows to a virtual standstill, allowing for a thorough study of the two characters and their environment. The narrator makes the reader conscious of time throughout the chapter. It was morning, he says, when he met his third master. In Guillén's excellent study, he points out that the disposition of time is simple, unilinear, and continuous, but that it changes tempo. In the first three chapters it moves slowly. This slowness is directly related to Lazarillo's suffering which seems never-ending. In the third chapter, however, there is a remarkable *ralenti* ("slowing of time"), counted hour by hour blending with Lazarillo's hopes and disappointments. There are instances when nothing seems to happen except the passing of time itself.[39] The narrator/protagonist is conscious of time and makes the reader aware of it also. It is morning when Lazarillo and his new master pass through the marketplace, but the Squire does not buy anything. Lazarillo surmises that he is not pleased with what he sees and will go elsewhere to shop. It is eleven o'clock when they enter the Cathedral, and Lazarillo watches the Squire devoutly attend Mass and the other divine services. They leave the church and begin to walk down a street very slowly. The clock strikes one when they come to a house. Up to this point the narrator makes the reader aware of the exact time of day when certain occurrences take place.

When they enter the house, the narrator turns to a description of both the house and the Squire. Through Lazarillo's observations

the author shows his masterful skill. Lazarillo, a protagonist now
nearing adolescence, is a keen observer of character and environment. When they cross the threshold Lazarillo describes the en-
trance as dark and *lóbrega* ("gloomy," "mournful," "associated
with death"), recognizing that it would frighten anyone who might
see it. The narrator then recounts how the Squire takes off his cape,
how he makes sure that his servant's hands are clean, and how the
cape is brushed and folded.[40] The Squire dusts off a bench and lays
his cape on it. After this he asks lengthy questions about Lazarillo's
past. The boy satisfies his master's curiosity by lying to the best of
his ability, telling him the good things and omitting the bad. When
this is over, time seems to slow down even more. Ever so slowly
Lazarillo begins to suspect that his master is not what he really appears to be. They sit in silence for a while. Lazarillo realizes that it is
nearly two o'clock and that his master "looked about as likely to
have a meal as a dead man." The house now appears to Lazarillo to
be "enchanted." While he is working this out in his mind, his
master finally asks if he has eaten. Of course, Lazarillo has not eaten
since he met the Squire, and that was before eight o'clock in the
morning. He tells him this. The Squire answers with a lie, affirming
that although it was quite early when they met, he had already
eaten. He says that he only takes one meal and does not expect to eat
again until evening. He tells Lazarillo "You will have to do as well
as you can. We will eat later on." When Lazarillo hears this he is
thunderstruck and filled with despair. In an emotional outburst addressed to "Your Grace," he unburdens some of his feelings:
"Your Grace can imagine that, when I heard him say this, I almost
fainted, not so much from hunger as from realizing for once and for
all how adverse my fortune really was."

Lazarillo's disillusionment has been a slow process, but now it
moves toward a climax. The protagonist links the hunger theme to
the trilogy. Lazarillo recalls his fears about leaving the priest, finding someone who is worse, and ending his miserable existence
altogether. Tarr believes that the close connection between this
passage, which refers to the Priest and to Lazarillo's almost certain
death, makes it evident that the author has been consciously working since the second chapter[41] on a definite climactic principle. In
the beginning of chapter 2, Lazarillo thought that he had gone
"from the frying pan into the fire." Now, this situation seems to be
the "fire." The author begins to set up a situation of climactic
despair as Lazarillo, after thinking of the Priest, says: "Finally, I

cried bitterly over my wretched past and my imminent future death." This thought of great pessimism and despair is shared with "Your Grace" and the reader. In this chapter most of the asides are snide remarks which Lazarillo makes concerning his master's pretensions. The emotional outbursts are most important, because they give the reader a valuable insight into Lazarillo's way of thinking. When the boy makes this remark concerning his past life and imminent death, he is mentally at his lowest point, but the climax of despair is yet to come.

The next scene shows the author's skill as he portrays a starving Squire who needs to eat but cannot abandon the role of a petty noble. He depicts a Lazarillo, no longer a child, who discerns illusions and has become a good judge of character. After the scene of hunger is set, Lazarillo beings to develop a sense of pity and charity and chooses to act out a role that enables the Squire to maintain his pretense and still eat.[42] Both servant and master pretend not to know what is going on; silence and deception preserve honor. Lazarillo tells his master not to worry about him. He is a boy who does not care too much about his belly. In fact, he has a very small stomach, and all of the masters he has had thus far have thought very highly of him for this reason. The Squire responds by saying that moderation is a virtue, and stuffing oneself is for pigs. In the first of six asides in this chapter, Lazarillo speaks his mind, and says sarcastically: "I have understood you well . . . damn the medicine and virtue that my masters found in being hungry." When Lazarillo begins to eat some bread that he has obtained by begging, the Squire takes the largest piece from the boy and comments on how good the bread looks. He then asks how Lazarillo got it and if it has been kneaded by clean hands. He begins to tear big chunks out of it and wolf it down. Lazarillo is the servant, and he addresses his master outwardly with the proper courtesy. The dialogue here is filled with social conventions and lies as the asides point out, but the characters subtly understand one another.[43] Lazarillo's sarcastic aside the others that follow show what he really thinks and by using the *tú* ("thou") form in the asides, Lazarillo brings the hypocritical Squire down to his level, that of a beggar. Inner thoughts are understood and outward appearances are preserved. With the author's use of dialogue, the asides, and Lazarillo's emotional outbursts, the two characters, their motives, and their values become evident to the reader.

The scene which follows is a preparation for Lazarillo's climax of mental anguish and despair. Together Lazarillo and his master prepare the Squire's miserable bed. The Squire declares that it is a long way to the market and that the road is dangerous in the evening, so he suggests they not go out to eat. He adds that he has not laid in any provisions, because he lives alone and eats out a lot, but tomorrow God will provide. Lazarillo tells him not to worry, that he knows how to put up with hunger for one night or more, if necessary. When the Squire says that he considers this a sign of good health, Lazarillo responds in another aside: "If that is the case . . . I will be unlucky enough to have to keep it all my life." There is quite a difference between what Lazarillo says and what he does. Outwardly he plays a role[44] and represses the horrible reality he has to face; inwardly he feels strong resentment, as the bitter sarcasm of his asides indicate, and his emotional outbursts mark his rage and despair. Master and servant go to bed, but Lazarillo has a sleepless night, and it is at this point that he confides in "Your Grace" and the reader his innermost feelings of utter hopelessness. Realizing now that there is no chance for improving his lot, he reaches the apex of despair, and in an emotional outburst which, for me, is unrivaled in Spanish literature in the intensity of its pessimism, he says:

I did not get much sleep, since the wooden slats of the bed and my bones quarreled violently all night long. What with my starvation and hardship there was not an ounce of flesh on my body. Besides I had eaten hardly anything that day, and hunger and sleep do not mix very well. I cursed myself (God forgive me) and my rotten fate time and time again that night; but worse, not daring to turn over so as not to wake him, many times I asked God for death.

This desire for God to end his miserable early existence, expressed not once but many times during the night, is, I believe, unique in Spanish literature in its sense of total despair. For Lazarillo there is no hope, and his rage and profound frustration are shared only with God, "Your Grace," and the reader. The narrator's point of view in this outburst is not that of a young boy but rather that of a pessimistic skeptic whose attitude takes shape here only to be hardened in the last chapter.

The morning after his sleepless night, Lazarillo, acting as valet, helps the Squire to wash and dress. The Squire that the author depicts here is not a stock type but a new creation. He is the Spanish

hidalgo ("noble") who esteems honor more than anything else
and, above all, wants to cut a good figure.[45] Lazarillo observes his
master's pretentious demeanor, his valued cape and sword, and his
swagger as he leaves the house, and he addresses God:

Lord . . . You give the sickness and then the medicine. Who could meet
my master and not think, seeing how happy he looks, that he has had sup-
per, slept in a comfortable bed, and although it is early in the morning,
has had a good lunch. Oh, Lord, You have great secrets that are unknown
to the common folk. . . .

These remarks are some of the protagonist's most intimate
thoughts. The God that he addresses is an inscrutable one.[46] This is
a God whose enigmatic plan and justice, if they exist, are simply not
understood by Lazarillo. The narrator's philosophical attitude of
skepticism is reflected in Lazarillo's attitude here.

At this point in the novel Lazarillo shares his innermost thoughts
with God and the reader. He sees how God allows suffering, and
the young boy is puzzled by this. Lazarillo observes the Squire's
false sense of pride and wonders aloud to God: "Oh Lord, how
many like him do you have scattered around the world that suffer
for the sake of wretched honor what they should not suffer for
You?" He sees through the hypocritical behavior of the Squire
whose primary social and personal value is that of illusory honor,[47]
but he does not expose him. Lazarillo as *histor* is a discerning
thinker, and he understands that the Squire too suffers. He too is
alone. The problem facing Lazarillo in this situation is to alleviate
both his own hunger and that of the Squire, and still allow his
master to maintain his dignity. This he does by playing a role. The
Squire gladly shares another meal with Lazarillo but asks that
nobody know that Lazarillo, who begs for food, is living with him.
It is a question of honor as he says. He blames his bad luck on his
house and says that within a month he will leave it. The two live
from hand-to-mouth for approximately ten days, and Lazarillo
reflects that he has escaped from his two previous masters only to
wind up with a dependent. Even so, Lazarillo confesses that he is
quite fond of the Squire, because, like him, the Squire has nothing
to his name and has no options.

Lazarillo is curious to know if the Squire is as poor as he seems,
and one morning when his master goes to a different part of the

house, Lazarillo searches his clothes and finds an empty purse. In this moment Lazarillo realizes that economically they are equals, and this realization establishes an intimacy between servant and master bound by adversity and suffering.[48] Lazarillo's other masters were at odds with him or outright adversaries; this one is a partner in starvation. In effect he is worse off than Lazarillo. Because of his pride and his social status, he can neither work with his hands nor beg. With the alms that the boy receives he relieves his hunger and feeds the Squire who has become dependent on his servant. The reality that the Squire has to face is so unbearable he creates a world of illusion as a defense mechanism. Lazarillo knows that the Squire has no options and says to himself: "This man . . . is poor and nobody gives him what he needs." He observes that the miserable Priest had a good position and the Blind Man a golden tongue, but they both starved him and deserved to be disliked. The Squire is different: "I pity him. As God is my witness, whenever I meet one of his type today walking with great pomp, I feel sorry for him and wonder if he is going through what I saw my master suffer."[49] Thus Lazarillo sees through his master but takes him on as a dependent and even becomes quite fond of him. No longer is Lazarillo a cunning rogue but rather a sensitive, charitable youth who understands a good bit about human behavior. Lazarillo observes that there are many like the Squire who do not have a penny to their name but have to keep up appearances, and they will never change.[50]

For some time Lazarillo helps the Squire to exist by giving him food. But adverse fortune strikes another blow. Because of a poor harvest, the Town Council decrees that poor people who are not natives of Toledo have to leave the city.[51] Lazarillo comments: "You can imagine, if you have any imagination at all, the abstinence and sadness we endured in silence." By stimulating the reader's imagination, Lazarillo's lack of description makes the suffering even more impressive. Master and servant spend two or three days without food. What are they to do? Their means of support is cut off. Like Huckleberry Finn and his companion Jim there is no place for them in society. Lazarillo is sorrier for the Squire than for himself: "I was not as sorry for myself as I was for my poor master who did not eat a bit of bread in a whole week. . . . And to see him walk down the street at lunch time with his head high like a pedigreed greyhound. And as for his wretched honor . . . he would stand in the doorway picking his teeth which had nothing stuck between them.'' The Squire invents a reason for his misfortune. He blames his ill luck on his sad and *lóbrega* (''gloomy'') house and says that since he has been there things have gone from bad to worse. However, by the end of the month he will leave; supposedly his luck will change.

At this point in the chapter the author inserts the episode of the funeral procession, based on folklore,[52] which binds the themes of hunger and death together and probably was meant to serve as comic relief.[53] The author has been preparing for this episode by the repetition, among other things, of the adjective *lóbrega* to describe the house. The Squire comes into some money and sends Lazarillo to the market to buy some wine. On the way the boy encounters a funeral procession, and he hears the widow shriek: ''Oh, my husband, where are they taking you? To the sad and unlucky house, to the dark and *lóbrega* (''gloomy'') house, to the house where there is nothing to eat or drink.'' Lazarillo has grown a bit and is wiser than he was, but he is still a boy, and the author here reminds us of that fact. When he hears this lamentation, Lazarillo thinks that they are bringing the body to the Squire's house and races home to warn him. The Squire, listening to the frightened boy's story, bursts into a fit of laughter, and ever afterward when he recalls Lazarillo's remarks, he roars with laughter, as the narrator tells us. The Squire is the only main character in the book to laugh, and this is the only mention of it.[54] The comic relief may have been meant for the character as well as the reader, who both need a release from the gloominess conveyed in this chapter.

At this juncture the narration changes. Up to now the narrator has given us a description of the Squire's mannerisms; now the reader will get to know about his past. His prehistory, which is in the form of a confession within a confession, as Guillén observes, explains the motives for his actions.[55] As the story within a story unfolds the reader acquires knowledge about class distinction in Spain from someone who is portrayed as having firsthand experience. The Squire is a self-exile from Old Castile who left his native land because of a point of honor. He did not want to take his hat off to a gentle neighbor of higher rank. Of course, Lazarillo does not comprehend his sense of honor nor the Squire's behavior. His master goes on a tirade, attacking the language and gestures of courtesy, and ends with an indictment of those nobles who hire squires. It seems that even when a squire gets a job he is put through the mill.

Lazarillo's master says that if he landed a job with a good gentleman he would be able to "tell him lies as well as anyone else and flatter him all the time. I would laugh at his jokes . . . I would never say anything to annoy him. I would tell the servants off where he could see me, and make it seem that I am concerned about anything to do with his comfort. . . . I could find out about other people and give him a full account of them." The Squire maintains that this is what rich men want. They do not like honest men in their houses; in fact they despise them. The Squire's account is not only a scathing attack on gentlemen and their way of life, it is a commentary on a whole social class of squires whose position as valet is prized for its obsequiousness. All in all it is a sad commentary on society, its masks, and its exigencies.

The Squire's story is interrupted by a couple who come into the house asking for the rent. He, in turn, asks them to return later for payment. When they do return, and Lazarillo realizes that he is alone in the house, he knows that the Squire has abandoned him. He has been betrayed and left to face the consequences of his master's actions. Thus ends the trilogy which is based on the hunger theme. Lazarillo left his first master, was thrown out by the second, and now he is abandoned by the third.

In this chapter the hunger theme reaches its climax and Lazarillo, the height of despair. A masterful use of narrative technique shows us how Lazarillo comes to realize slowly that the Squire is not really what he pretends to be, and during this process of realization, the boy begins to understand the reason for his master's way of life. The author demonstrates his expertise in developing psychologically two characters who are socially incompatible but who are bound together by circumstances and by their mutual desire to improve their lot. Both hope to better their fortunes by changing geographical location, but their hopes and dreams end only in despair and disillusionment.

Chapter 4

The brevity of chapters 4 through 6 and their difference in style have puzzled critics and been a fertile source of inquiry and interpretation.[56] Chapter 4 is the most mysterious of the three. It is the shortest, only ninety-eight words, and deals with controversial material. The narrator may prefer not to recount his experience in detail here, and that, of course, remains his prerogative. He not only chooses the material he wishes to include in the narration but determines its length and style as well. A detailed description of the nefarious relationship between Lazarillo and the monk of the Order of Mercy might have been unprintable; in fact this episode was expurgated in the 1573 edition. Some critics believe the chapter is incomplete, and that an editor or censor may have removed the objectionable material from it. Others hold that the chapter merely serves as a transition and conforms to the style of the rest of the book. It could be that the chapter is brief for artistic reasons. Some scholars consider chapter 4–6 to be a triptych, and the two brief chapters 4 and 6 to be lateral panels for the longer chapter 5. The two brief chapters possibly serve to accelerate the passage of time as the story moves toward its denouement in chapter 7. Perhaps the narrator simply refuses to give "Your Grace" an "entire account" of himself as he promised in the prologue, choosing instead to remain silent for reasons of self-interest or protection. Whatever the reason, and whatever the interpretation, this fourth chapter, because of the delicate material it treats and because of its style and use of language, begs interpretation even from the less experienced.

There is a difference between what the epigraph of this chapter announces: "How Lázaro took a position with a monk of the Order of Mercy and what happened while in his service," and what actually takes place in the narrative.[57] The very first sentence of the chapter contains material that links it closely to the previous sentence, that is, the final sentence of chapter 3: "I had to look for a fourth one, and he turned out to be a monk of the Order of Mercy; the women I mentioned sent me to him. They said that he was a relative of theirs." The antecedent for "el cuarto" ("the fourth one") is Lazarillo's third master who is mentioned in the previous sentence. It seems, moreover, that this first line is meant also to introduce material that serves as a transition between the third and fifth chapters. In any case, this is not the first time that transitional material has preceded the introduction to a new master.

The monk is identified as a member of the Order of Mercy, a monastic order that dealt chiefly with the redemption of captives and was noted for its scandalous behavior especially in the New World.[58] The narrator tells that *mujercillas* ("little women") called the monk their relative. The diminutive suggests that the women were of ill repute, and the word *pariente* ("relative") has sexual connotations.[59] The sentences which follow continue to describe the monk:

He was not very fond of singing in the choir and eating in the monastery, but loved to attend to secular affairs, to go out and to visit people. So much so, that he used to wear out more shoes than the rest of his community put together. He gave me the first pair of shoes that I ever wore out. They did not last me eight days; I could not stand his running around anymore. So, for this reason, and for other "little things" I will not mention, I left him.

Thus ends this brief chapter which I have included here in its entirety.

Although brief, the chapter is charged with innuendo. *Mujercillas* call this man their *pariente,* and we learn that he has an interest in "secular affairs." The author's use of euphemism and his very conciseness produce a highly suggestive understatement. The euphemism says a great deal while ostensibly hiding what the narrator, for his own reasons, chooses not to describe openly. The Monk's love of secular affairs become dubious here as does his *trote* ("running around"). *Trote* and the word *convento* ("monastery") suggest Lazarillo's role as a *trotaconventos* ("go-between"; literally, "a convent-trotter").[60] The words and the role recall the not insignificant fact that *trotaconventos* is the famous panderer in Juan Ruiz's *El libro de buen amor* (*The Book of Good Love*). Thus, the narrator first alludes to the scandalous behavior of the Monk by identifying him as a member of the Order of Mercy; then he discreetly enlarges upon the Monk's illicit activities through the use of metaphor and euphemism.

The narrator has obviously selected with great care the material that he includes here, and he deals with it in the same fashion, so that he himself may not be in the Monk's affairs. The use of the imperfect tense to describe the Monk's wearing out of many shoes indicates the frequency and habitual nature of his actions.[61] Lazarillo's shoes last only eight days, which underlines his own hurried intensity of activity as servant to this master. The final sentence is pregnant with innuendo. The *cosillas* ("little things") which caused Lazarillo to leave the Monk are left for the reader to interpret. Lazarillo, up to this point, has endured quite a bit from his masters, and for him to leave this one of his own free will leads the reader to suspect unthinkable behavior. The narrator's silence, his refusal to give "Your Grace" "an entire account" of this affair, may well imply that the "little things" refer to the unspeakable crime, namely, homosexual activity.[62] Of course, the reader's attention is focused on Lazarillo's relationship with the Monk by the mere fact that the narrator chooses to censor the material and tell the reader he is doing so. This clever device tempts the reader who has a fertile imagination to imagine the worst.

The concise and incriminating description of the Monk is complete in itself even though much—the other "little things"—is omitted. Tarr points out other parts in the novel where the author is reticent to tell all that he saw or experienced.[63] Chapter 4 is essentially a single paragraph which the narrator himself saw fit to censor; as transitional material, it is similar to the beginnings of the second and third chapters and serves as an interval between two masters.

Chapter 5

The fourth chapter, written completely in the third person, ended with the narrator's choosing to withhold information. In the fifth, the narrator will tell all that he knows and except for the first forty-three lines and the last forty, will again use the third person.[64] The central figure of chapter 5 is a pardoner, a stock literary type who, like Masuccio's Brother Girolamo and Boccaccio's Brother Onion, uses trickery and cunning to fleece religious believers. Almost all of this chapter is dedicated to the deception that he and a constable perpetrate, and Lázaro is more of an observer than a protagonist here.

Some critics believe that the source for this episode is Masuccio's fourth *novella,* while others opt for the Flemish version of *Liber vagatorum* or the early Spanish translation of *The Golden Ass.* Ricapito argues persuasively for Masuccio's *novella*; however, the author of *Lazarillo de Tormes* did not merely imitate the story but rather reworked and adapted it to fit a particular Spanish social situation.[65] Such practice falls well within the Renaissance literary tradition.

An examination of the similarities between the two stories will show how the author of *Lazarillo de Tormes* adapted the material to suit his own artistic creation. The Italian tale begins with a description of corrupt clergymen and their shameless behavior. The story is about Brother Girolamo of Spoleto who takes a well-preserved bone and, with the aid of his cohort Brother Mariano, contends that it is from the arm of the Evangelist Saint Luke. Their fraud is effected, of course, by deceit. Mariano, dressed as a Dominican, accuses Girolamo of tricking the religious believers. In response, Girolamo asks for God for a miracle and with that his accomplice falls to the ground in a fit. Girolamo then offers up prayers and gives Mariano a glass of water containing a piece of the relic's fingernail. This revives Mariano. The pair reap great profit from their trick and continue their journey to Calabria where they perpetrate more frauds. Masuccio ends with an epilogue denouncing those clergymen who commit the base act of deceiving God and man.

The author of *Lazarillo de Tormes* presents a different version of this plot, substituting the bone with a *bula* ("papal bull"), and Fra Girolamo and his friend, with a pardoner and a constable. Pardoners and papal indulgences were topics of great concern in Spain during the Renaissance. Pardoners of the Holy Crusade sold indulgences granting remission of sins to those who purchased the bulls. The money that they collected supposedly funded the campaign against the infidels. The bulls were documents issued by the pope and sealed with a *bulla,* a round seal affixed to the bull itself. The sale of these bulls brought a goodly profit to the state. The pardoners were paid a commission, and entrepreneurial, unscrupulous ones made a great deal of money.

Chapter 5 opens with the narrator's description of his master, the Pardoner, as a wretched and brazen man. Indeed, this Pardoner stands out among others; they are bad, but he is worse, for he is the most unscrupulous and shameless man that Lázaro has ever seen or hopes to see. Lázaro himself is no angel, so his master must really be a rogue. The succinct but biting description of the Pardoner is written in the first person. The narrator/protagonist then separates himself from his master by using the third person and taking a position of innocent observer. Here, Lázaro as *histor* retains his distance and control over what he observes and judges. The story is presented to "Your Grace" and to the reader in direct narration. Lázaro is associated with the innocent people in the chapter who are tricked by the Pardoner. The setting of the story is a village near Toledo. The Pardoner has been there for two or three days and has not sold a single bull. What is more, it does not look as if the natives have any intention of buying any. These skeptical people are not easily taken in, and their adversary relationship with the Pardoner not only sets the scene for his trick but emphasizes his perverted talent.

One night while the Pardoner is playing cards a quarrel ensues between him and another unsavory character, an *alguacil* ("constable").[66] Among other things the Constable accuses the Pardoner of being a fraud, and says publicly that the bulls he is trying to sell are counterfeit. The next day, while the Pardoner is delivering a convincing sermon[67] from the pulpit in the local church, the Constable enters and accuses him of being a swindler. It is at this moment that the Pardoner prays to God for a miracle and the Constable falls convulsively to the floor. The Pardoner descends from the pulpit, places a bull on the Constable's head, and implores God to return the sinner to health. With that the "sinner" comes to his senses. The people believe this to be a miracle, and they purchase many bulls from the Pardoner. The author emphasizes the craftiness of the Pardoner by including Lázaro among those who are duped. It is only when Lázaro sees his master and the Constable laughing together that he comes to understand that the whole incident had been planned by the crafty Pardoner.

By allowing Lázaro to be taken in by the Pardoner, the author also emphasizes the distance between the master and his servant. The shameful Pardoner is a skilled practioner of deceit, and he and the Constable are consummate actors. The disengagement of the narrator allows the story to develop uninterrupted. This episode is different from others in the novel in that it could stand on its own as an independent entity. It almost seems to be an interpolation deliberately placed here to direct the narrative away from the hunger theme that has ruled the servant/master relationship up to this point.

The story is a distinctly Spanish rendering of a contemporary problem. The corruption manifested in the selling of bulls was a bitter controversial issue at the time of the book's publication. There were various types of bulls allowed in Spain, but those of the Holy Crusade were the most popular, hence the most lucrative.[68] Some of the profit went to the Royal Treasury and some went to the Church. Of course the commission went to the pardoners. The system produced unscrupulous pardoners and numerous abuses as evidenced by the laws which were passed regarding their sale. The

abuses were denounced in many meetings of the Parliament including the one that took place in 1525. In 1524, Charles V issued a
decree forbidding preachers to coerce people to buy bulls against
their will and prohibiting the punishment of those who did not attend sermons.[69] This law was renewed in 1528 and 1554, which
means that the abuses most certainly continued. The series of
decrees actually gave civil authorities great power, and they in turn
began to extract payment for those same bulls. There was a threat of
excommunication if people did not buy them. The bulls were also
believed to alleviate the sins of the living as well as the dead. So
much value accrued to the bulls that they became a form of paper
currency which the government exchanged for coin. Communities
that purchased them were simply paying another form of
taxation.[70]

In an artistic manner, the author of *Lazarillo de Tormes* portrays a
well-known social problem of the time.[71] The targets of his satire in
this chapter are illusory religious values, the worthless bull, the in-
sincere sermon, and the false miracle. He first exaggerates the skepticism and unwillingness of the people from the village to buy bulls.
Then he presents the Pardoner's speech which follows a pattern of
forensic oration. The author is skillful in reproducing oral language
in a realistic way. The Pardoner's words are as convincing as his actions. Even Lázaro, the experienced *pícaro,* is duped by this man's
artful plan and his rhetorical prowess. Nowhere in the novel is the
art of persuasion more poignantly depicted. Here the author has
portrayed a situation that both reflects and seeks to change social
values of the Spain of the 1550s. At the end of the chapter, Lazarillo
returns to the foreground, tells the reader how impressed he was by
the trick and reflects to himself: "I wonder how many others there
are like this one swindling innocent people." Lázaro then says that
he stayed with the Pardoner for almost four months, and although
he ate well, he also suffered some hard times, and so, he decided to
leave this master.

Chapter 6

Lázaro's misfortunes and his dramatic battle against hunger reach
their peak in chapter 3. After that the author accelerates the passage

of time, bringing Lazarillo's childhood and adolescence to an end and preparing the reader for the denouement in the last chapter. Lázaro spends only eight days with the Monk of the Order of Mercy and four months with the Pardoner. His adolescence and apprenticeship are over. Now the people he works for are employers, not masters.

The sixth chapter, like the fourth, is very short, consisting of some twenty lines. It, too, serves as a rapid transition, this time into the world of commerce. Lázaro's first employer, an artist who paints tambourines, is discussed in one sentence. The young man's job is to mix paints, and, as might well be expected by now, he suffers many difficulties with the painter. He has still not been able to obtain the good life. Next, a chaplain provides him with a donkey, four jugs, and a whip in order to sell water. Now he enters the world of commerce, selling water on a commission basis and sharing some of the profits with the chaplain. He is happy about this position and describes it as "the first step that I climbed to reach the *good* life . . ." (my italics). He saves money from his earnings and, after four years, buys the accoutrements he thinks necessary for social prestige. In a word, he becomes a consumer: "I did so well at the job that after four years I saved enough from my earnings to dress honorably in secondhand clothes; I bought an old fustian jacket (*jubón de fustán viejo*), worn coat (*sayo raído*) with braided sleeves and an open collar, a cape which once had a fringe, and an old sword made in Cuellar." Lázaro buys the goods which for him represent honor. After the episode of the Squire, both Lázaro and the reader know that clothes do not make the man, that the cape and sword, which were considered by some to be worthwhile, are illusory goods of fortune. The hypocrisy of the Squire, which he once criticized, he now emulates. Dressed in this manner, he describes himself as an "hombre de bien" ("an affluent man"), a man who is well off, and he believes that he has "arrived." And so he has.

When one looks closely at how he describes his clothes, one sees that the author seems to separate himself from his protagonist, and using irony in a special way, seems to actually ridicule him. Sieber notes the special use of irony here in his comparison between the narrator's description of these clothes and those of the Squire.[72] He points out that Lázaro buys a replica of the Squire's costume and draws the reader's attention to it as he describes each article in detail. When Lázaro first meets the Squire, he observes that he is

dressed well in *calzas* ("stockings"), a *jubón* ("jacket"), a *sayo*
("coat") and a *capa* ("cape"). Now Lázaro duplicates the Squire's
wardrobe, but, as he describes each piece, he denigrates it. The
newly "successful" young man buys an *old* jacket . . . and an *old*
sword. For Sieber the irony here seems to extend beyond Lázaro and
"Your Grace." If anyone is laughing, he believes it is the author
who is laughing at his character and his readers. The first step of the
social ladder that Lázaro has just climbed is a low one, but it is
nonetheless just another illusion.

Chapter 7

"I would also like those people who are proud of being high born
to realize how little this means, since Fortune smiled on them, and
how much more worthy are those who have suffered misfortune,
but by dint of effort and cunning, have rowed and reached a good
port." So, as we recall, ends the prologue which promises to show
how the protagonist will combat adverse fortune and achieve success. Yet, the narrator does not give a "complete account" of
himself as he says he will. Instead he chooses the episodes he wants
to narrate, revealing or hiding the truth about them through the
skillful and ironic use of language. In chapter 7 the author concludes Lázaro's story and answers the questions that the reader has
had up to this point. Who is "Your Grace?" What is the *caso*
("affair") that he supposedly has an interest in? Why is it being explained and partly justified? What is the "good port" that the protagonist finally reaches by dint of effort and cunning? Is it a success
story or is Lázaro's success just another illusion governed by Fortune? All of these questions are answered in chapter 7, but the narrator uses the same ironic language he has used throughout the
book, and thus both reveals and dissimulates, leaving the reader to
interpret the truth of the matter for himself.

Chapter 7 begins with the same transitional material as the earlier
ones and is linked with the previous chapter. The first part of the
chapter consists of a four-sentence description of Lázaro's job with a
constable. "After leaving the Chaplain I worked for a Constable.
But I did not stay long with him because in my view the job was
dangerous." Lázaro describes a scene in which some fugitives catch

the Constable and give him a good beating, which he manages to escape. That dangerous episode is enough for him to break his contract, for Lázaro is the antithesis of the chivalric hero who willingly faces danger. He is a practical person who wants to land a good job and survive as best he can.

The narrative continues as Lázaro thinks of settling down to an easy life and earning some money for his old age. Suddenly, "God enlightened me and guided me along a profitable path. And with lots of favors from friends and gentlemen, the hardships of my past were compensated for when I got the job I wanted. It was a Civil Service job. Only those who have one thrive." It seems at this point that his situation has taken a decided turn for the better. In a rare show of optimism the narrator speaks positively about his steady and secure job with the government. However, he landed this job with the help of friends. Who are these friends? At what price did he buy their favor? The author does not answer these questions; they are left to the reader's imagination. Yet Lázaro does add that one cannot get by without a government job. The tone of sarcasm which begins with this sentence is present throughout the chapter and culminates with the last sentence, a bitter statement on the protagonist's prosperity.

At first it appears that Lázaro has become "un hombre de bien" ("an affluent man") with a worthwhile and respectable position, but as the narrator continues his description of the job, the reader realizes that this is not the case. Again the narrator has dissimulated through euphemism. Lázaro's job is to make public announcements of wines. He also accompanies prisoners who, as he says, suffer persecution under justice,[73] and he announces their crimes. Finally, he reveals the truth: "In plain Spanish I am a town crier." Describing his position in this way, Lázaro avoids the truth as long as he can before confessing that he is a lowly town crier. The position of town crier was held to be so loathsome that only the basest types took that kind of job. One of the crier's duties was to assist the hangman. And so the successful position, about which Lázaro boasts, is not at all what it seems to be—a respectable Civil Service job.

Lázaro continues to describe his position by saying that he deals with wine and that he has been prosperous. If anyone sells wine or anything else in the city it passes through his hands, and, of course, he receives a cut from the take. He does so well that he draws the at-

tention of an Archpriest who becomes his last "protector": "At
that time the Archpriest of Saint Salvador, my master and Your
Grace's friend, heard about me, and saw how sharp-witted I was so
he arranged for me to marry a maid of his." It seems that the Blind
Man's prophecy ("if anybody is going to be lucky with wine in this
world, it will be you") has come true. Lázaro has exhibited such
talent in announcing wines and arranging business deals that he has
won the good auspices of the Archpriest, and earned himself a
bride. This is not a marriage based on love or designed for pro-
creation; it is strictly an economic arrangement. Lázaro says: "Seeing that only advantages and good could come from being
associated with such a person I agreed to get married, and to this day
I have not regretted it . . . the Archpriest takes good care of us."
The narrator brings the time of the story to the present, so that the
time of the narration now coincides with that of the last paragraph
of the prologue: "Your Grace has written and asked me to tell him
of the affair in detail so I thought I would start at the beginning . . .
so that you would have a complete account of my life." At last, the
narrator explains what the "affair" is, but in no way has he given a
"complete account" of his life.

Lázaro comments on his marriage in favorable terms, saying that
the priest shows great kindness to husband and wife by giving them
provisions and clothes and arranging for the couple to live next door
to him. However, the marriage, like the Civil Service position, is not
really what it appears to be. Certainly it seems that Lázaro has struck
up an arrangement with the priest because of his talents as a town
crier, and the Archpriest seems to be a protector who looks kindly on
the couple. But language again has camouflaged the truth. The
neighbors know that something is amiss, and Lázaro reveals this:
"But evil tongues, that are never lacking, make life impossible for
us, saying I don't know what I do know what ("*no sé qué y sí sé
qué*") about my wife's going to make his (the Archpriest's) bed and
cook his meals. . . ." Lázaro has what he describes as a nagging
suspicion concerning his wife's fidelity. In fact, he knows exactly
what is going on. The mystery of the "affair" and why "Your
Grace" is interested in knowing about it is beginning to come to
light, while the novel, as an account of Lázaro's life, is becoming cir-
cular in form.

Whereas his mother had an affair in order to support a family,
Lázaro shares his wife with the Archpriest for material benefit. The

author thus debases marriage and the lustful habits of a member of the clergy at the same time. The *uxor dotata* theme of the husband's dependency on his wife's dowry and the theme of the lustful adulterous clergyman were not new to literature; the former appeared in the Latin comedy of Plautus, and the latter was popular in the Middle Ages. The originality of the cuckold and *uxor dotata* theme here is that Lázaro is the protagonist / narrator and, as such, he not only explains these matters, but lives them. The reason given for the explanation of the "affair" is that "Your Grace" has asked for it. Thus, the author has established a narrative in which the last chapter is linked with the prologue, and the subject matter of the whole novel is ultimately part of the explanation of the "affair."

Continuing his description of the marriage, the narrator has the Archpriest speak to Lázaro telling him that he should not be surprised if people gossip about his wife's comings and goings. The priest advises Lázaro not to heed the neighbors' gossip. Instead he should look out for himself and pay attention to what is profitable for him. Lázaro's response to the cynical priest shows that he has followed his mother's example: "Señor . . . yo determiné de arrimarme a los buenos." ("Sir . . . I decided to associate with the good people"). These are almost the exact words used to describe his mother's mode of survival. She, because of dire circumstances, "determinó arrimarse a los buenos para ser uno dellos" ("decided to associate with the good people in order to become one of them"). The gossipers may ruin Lázaro's profitable arrangement, a source of good fortune for him, and they are not to be heeded. Indeed, they must be silenced in order for the arrangement to continue. By having the priest suggest the arrangement and the strategy of silence, the narrator reduces Lázaro's active participation in the matter. Lázaro is well aware of the rumors which are circulating, and his remarks to the Archpriest emphasize their veracity: "It is true that my friends have told me some things about my wife. In fact they have certified to me that she had three children before she married me." Not only have his friends talked to him about his wife's affair, but they have *certified* that she has given birth three times. Lázaro knows the truth as well as the Archpriest and his wife. And when the Archpriest says that Lázaro's wife enters and leaves his house with honor, he is lying. He sees these rumors as possibly harmful financially for Lázaro and suggests an exchange: honor for profit. When Lázaro says: "I decided to associate with the good people," the pact is sealed and the exchange has been made. These bitter, cynical words form the agreement, which will be maintained by silence. After hearing Lázaro's remarks concerning the rumors, his wife begins to swear such fearful oaths that he thinks the house will cave in. She cries, screams, and curses the man who brought them together. She is a good example of the guilty person whose strategy is that a good offense is a good defense. In this case she is right. Lázaro is on the defensive when he says: "I began to wish that I were dead and had never said a word. But between my master and me we talked to her and made her so many promises that she stopped crying. I swore to her that as long as I lived I would never mention a word about that matter and that I was happy about her and felt good about her entering and leaving his house night and day, since I was sure of her *goodness*" (my italics).

There is a melancholy tone of bitterness and resignation in Lázaro's words as he describes how he keeps "peace" in his house. The bitterness and sarcasm increase as the chapter progresses until it culminates in the last sentence of the book. Silence is the key to maintaining this type of arrangement, and Lázaro has maintained it till the present time of narration: "Until today no one has heard us mention the affair. In fact, when I sense that someone wants to say something to me about her I cut him short and say: 'Look, if you are my friend do not say anything to upset me, because anyone who annoys me is no friend of mine.'" His statement leaves no doubt that the affair has been going on for some time. Lázaro silences his friends, thereby trading friendship for silence. Without the silence Lázaro might lose his privileged position. In the long run it is profitable for him not to "see" and to keep his friends from speaking of the "affair." He even threatens his friends with violence if they speak and thus maintains "peace" in his household. He continues to comment in a sarcastic manner on his wife's "goodness," vouching for it by swearing (falsely) on the Holy Eucharist.[74] He thanks God for such a wonderful woman, and says: "I would swear on the Sacred Host that she is as *good* a woman as any in Toledo" (my italics). If Lázaro's wife is as good as any in Toledo, one can only imagine what the other women are like and what the worst would be like.[75]

From the narrator's perspective, Lázaro's marriage is a joke. His depiction of it reflects a cynical and critical view of marriage as a social and religious institution. Lázaro abandons the Christian precepts of marriage, and his attitude toward his wife and their relationship is the exact opposite of the idealistic love portrayed in chivalric romances of the day. He keeps peace with his "ideal" wife through threats of violence against those who might reveal the truth. Silence is imposed and maintained. No one says anything about the "affair," and Lázaro keeps peace in his house. He has become one of the "good" people that he has described throughout the book.

In this chapter hypocrisy reigns supreme.[76] Lázaro claims that his arrangement is good and profitable, but it is really an untenable situation; yet all who know about it must remain silent. He, like the Squire, decides to live the life of illusion, of false success and pretended happiness. He is a cynical skeptic, who chooses to wear the mask of the hypocritical society which he has observed and to join that society (even if only partially) whose values he does not esteem. Lázaro is in this position because there is no viable alternative for him, or so he thinks.

The last two sentences of the novel have provoked a good deal of speculation and interpretation because of their content and the change in tenses. The first is: "Esto fue el mismo año que nuestro victorioso Emperador en esta insigne ciudad de Toledo entró, y tuvo en ella Cortes, y se hicieron grandes regocijos, y fiestas, como Vuestra Merced habrá oído." ("This was the same year that our victorious emperor entered this famous city of Toledo and held his Parliament here, there were great festivities as Your Grace no doubt has heard.") Besides the brusque change from the present tense to the preterite, there is a break in the internal logic of the work. The two sentences seem to refer to a remote past which "Your Grace" must have heard of. Ayala notices an incongruence here because of the tense change and believes that these two sentences could have been added to the first edition by an editor.[77] "The same year that our victorious emperor . . . held Parliament . . ." could refer to either the Parliament of 1525, which occurred shortly after the Battle of Pavia where Charles V was victorious, or to the Parliament of 1538 that dealt, among other things, with the Erasmian polemic of the time, and which was also followed by festivities.[78] With this sentence Lázaro sarcastically likens his "success" to that of the Spanish Empire. He is a lowly town crier who relates his dishonor to its honor and glory. He is now part of and reflects a decadent society that is hypocritical, impoverished, unstable, chaotic, unfeeling, and in a state of moral decay. He has managed to succeed within its structure and its value system by trading his honor for material good. Lázaro's remarks could, on the other hand, be a malicious commentary on the Emperor Charles who, after 1550, was at the helm of a troubled and decadent empire. By dint of the sarcastic comparison Lázaro brings the emperor down to his own level.

The book does not end here. There is one more sentence, even more sarcastic than the two previous ones: "Pues en este tiempo estaba en mi prosperidad y en la cumbre de buena fortuna." ("At that time I was prosperous and at the summit of *good* fortune" [my italics]). The story of Lázaro's life represents the moral decay and material progress of a human being who at first is betrayed by appearances and later accepts them as a way of life. His unfortunate life is compared to a Spain defeated at Los Gelves, a Spain whose mission against the Moors had become perverted, a Spain which warred against fellow Christians. His life, like the Spanish Empire, is marked by apparent glory but authentic ruin. With sarcastic resignation, Lázaro accepts his final decadent status as irrevocable. The author may be doing the same with Spain's fate during the 1550s.

The narrator's attitude and point of view are essential to a thorough understanding of the work and its tone. They influence what he observes and interprets, and the manner in which he does so. Lázaro's philosophical attitude toward society and his ethics are that of the wise philosophical skeptic who rejects the existence of certitudes and maintains, therefore, that objective validity is indemonstrable. Since it is impossible, according to this view, to attain to truth or even to certainty, Lázaro, like the wise skeptic, accepts as a rule of conduct the complete abstention from or suspension of judgment. What holds true for this ethical view applies equally to his social values, which are exemplified in his acceptance of his marital arrangement. Lázaro does not judge as protagonist or narrator; however, the reader is free to do so. In practical matters, Lázaro abandons himself to the customs of the time with passive tranquillity. According to the skeptical school of philosophy, the refusal to judge, with its concomitant adherence to society's rules, is supposed to bring tranquillity of the soul. At the end of the novel the only way that Lázaro can achieve peace is by telling his friends not to tell him anything that upsets him. In his ethical position Lázaro the narrator is a skeptic.

His metaphysical outlook, if he has one, is that the world is ruled by Fortune, and the only way that the less fortunate can survive, that is to say, "arrive at a good port," is by using "effort and cunning." There seem to be no acceptable first principles for Lázaro, and no moral basis for society. There exist no certitudes. His success or pseudosuccess is a fickle one, since it, like everything else, depends on Fortune and may disappear at any time. When Lázaro describes his "affair" and says that he is at the summit of good fortune, he is obviously not as happy as he pretends to be. As the proverb says: "a happy person has no story to tell."

Chapter Six
Narrative Technique
Autobiographical Style

Studies on the sources of the author's autobiographical style have proved to be more fruitful than those on the authorship, because they have contributed valuable insights into the novel. With regard to style, the first-person narrative has drawn the attention of many critics. Some have merely pointed out that precedents such as Juan Ruiz's *El libro de buen amor* (*The Book of Good Love*) are similar in form to *Lazarillo de Tormes*, or that the novel could be related to memoirs and autobiographies of the Renaissance. There is some similarity to the autobiographies and memoirs of this period, but as Lázaro Carreter points out in his excellent study of the autobiographical style of *Lazarillo de Tormes*,[1] their similarity does not mean that they served as a model for the novel. He goes beyond demonstrating the similarities of the *Lazarillo* to other autobiographies and studies the novelty of the author's autobiographical style. Américo Castro suggests that a biography of such an unimportant person would have lacked justification during the Renaissance, and the author probably stayed in the background for that reason, yielding the foreground to the narrator.[2] Castro believes that the autobiographical style is thus inseparable from the author's intention to bring to light the story of an insignificant person heretofore nonexistent or scorned. The author, a New Christian of Jewish origin, probably sought to protect himself, and withdrew so much that he did not even reveal his name. Thus, in Castro's view the autobiographical style of *Lazarillo de Tormes* is inseparable from its anonymity. His argument regarding the anonymity is convincing. This view is accepted by some critics, notably Lázaro Carreter, who finds Castro's thoughts on this matter convincing and concludes that the autobiography was an internal necessity with regard to style.

Marcel Bataillon, in his indispensable introduction to *Lazarillo de Tormes*, studies autobiographical literature, its origins, and its possible relationship to the novel. Autobiographical prose, some of which might have influenced *Lazarillo de Tormes*, appeared in Spain around 1550, in diverse genres, for example, the *Abencerraje* of Villegas, *Isea* by Núñez de Reinoso, and *Viaje de Turquía* (*Voyage from Turkey*), probably by Andrés Laguna. However, Bataillon believes that all of the precedents that one can recall, including *The Golden Ass* (*Metamorphoses*) of Apuleius—translated at that time by López de Cortegana—and the *Book of Good Love* of the Archpriest of Hita, are pale in comparison to *Lazarillo de Tormes*, which was the most advanced autobiographical work of the Spanish Renaissance.[3] Lázaro Carreter acknowledges that *Lazarillo de Tormes* makes use of the abundant folkloric sources and adds to Bataillon's examples of autobiographical prose work of Erasmian tendencies *El Crotalón* and the *Diálogo de las transformaciones* (*Dialogue of Transformations*), both published after the novel. Castro, Bataillon, and later Gilman emphasize the autobiographical element of the novel as essential to the work.[4] They consider the anonymity of the *Lazarillo de Tormes* to be an internal essence.

Although there were works at this time as daring as the novel which were not censured, the anonymity of the author could have been deliberate because of certain risks he might incur. It is very possible that the author did not want to be identified with the novel because it would have prejudiced the position he occupied, or because it would have been propitious for the Inquisition, which, in 1559, found certain parts of the book offensive, to call attention to the work during the time of the Erasmian polemic, since the novel seems to contain some influence of Erasmus. Several authors, including Erasmians, were experimenting with innovative forms of narrative.

Although some of the austere Erasmians rejected the Milesian tales as odious, it was Diego López, himself an Erasmian canon and inquisitor, who first translated *The Golden Ass* into Spanish. Erasmian didactic moral literature, which appeared mostly in the form of Lucianesque dialogues, was meant to be critical and corrective. Furthermore, it was intended to be truthful and useful as opposed to the idealistic literature of knights, ladies, and shepherds. As some Erasmians experimented with new narrative forms such as the novel of transformations and dialogues, their didacticism gave way to mere entertainment. This literature, written about the time

Lazarillo de Tormes was first published, possibly influenced the novel.

The Golden Ass of Apuleius most certainly had an influence on the structure of *Lazarillo de Tormes*. It is a first-person narrative in which Lucias, who is turned into an ass, recounts his many adventures. He serves several masters, observes the seamy side of life, and narrates the many calamities that befall him. In the history of narrative, *The Golden Ass*, as first-person narrative, established the pattern of inward journey as apology, and the *Confessions* of Augustine, the inward journey as confession. Both were mimetic, and both, I maintain, influenced picaresque fiction and *Lazarillo de Tormes*. In the *Confessions,* written long after his conversion, Augustine sets down for the benefit of others the story of his early life and his conversion to Christianity. His is the first authentic ancient autobiography, and the description of his youth is the only detailed account of the childhood of a great man which antiquity has left us. Both *The Golden Ass* and the *Confessions* are narratives in which the protagonist observes accurately, has keen perception, and in the end is converted.

Lazarillo de Tormes exhibits a mixture of rhetoric and realism similar to that of *The Golden Ass*. In both books there is a great emphasis on desire on the part of the protagonist, and their rhetorical and realistic art arouses in the reader a sense of human warmth, intimacy, and sympathy for the protagonist. They both have a glaringly graphic realism which is, at times, humorous, pitiful, and even grotesque. This realism lends itself to the satire and irony also present in both works. In the *Confessions* Augustine's observations of reality reveal a more militant attitude toward the vices and cruelty (see his view of his friend Alpius in chapter 8, book 6). The transition from the old world to the new can be seen in his analytical voyage through scattered islands, the mysticism of the Manichees, the skepticism of the Academic philosophers, and the fatalism of the astrologers until he at last finds his place in the Church. The autobiographical classics observed the realities of their time and reveal a militant attitude in Augustine and a satirical one in Apuleius.

Autobiographical fiction could be directed to the reader (*Isea*), to another character within the narration (*Abindarráez*), or to an addressee of the written material (*Cárcel de Amor* [*The Jail of Love*]) in the form of letters. *Lazarillo de Tormes* pertains to the third group. It is a spoken epistle, as Guillén has pointed out,[5] written by a town crier from Toledo to "Your Grace," a friend of the Archpriest who appears in the seventh chapter. Apparently "Your Grace" is interested in the marital arrangement that Lázaro has with his wife and the Archpriest, and we, the readers, overhear Lázaro's confession to the friend of his protector. In the prologue, Lázaro presents himself as writer and speaks as such. Then, at a given moment in chapter 7 the receiver of the epistle appears as a character, a friend of the Archpriest whom Lázaro addresses: "At that time the Archpriest of Saint Salvador, and Your Grace's friend, heard about me and noticed how able and sharp-witted I was, because I used to announce that his wines were for sale. So he arranged for me to marry a servant of his."

The narrator of the novel is the adult Lázaro who relates his pseudoautobiography in letter form, while the protagonist in most of the narrative is Lazarillo as a boy, who is much more *simpático,* entertaining, and impressive than the adult Lázaro. Most readers cannot help but identify with Lazarillo, the boy, and it is for this reason that he has received most of the attention of critics and artists. However, with regard to the novelistic technique of the work, it is Lázaro the man who plays the more important role. It is Lázaro the adult who has been asked by "Your Grace," friend of the Archpriest, to write an account of the affair, that is, Lázaro's marital arrangement which evidently interested him. In the prologue Lázaro says: "Your Grace has written me and asked me to write and tell about the affair in detail, so I thought I would start at the beginning, not in the middle, so that Your Grace would have a complete account of my life."

The letter is in effect the book, and Lázaro, the adult, is the narrator telling his story at the time that he is town crier in the narration. We, as second readers of the letter, are eavesdroppers, so to speak, and the affair that he refers to is the three-way arrangement that Lázaro, his wife, and the Archpriest have. Lázaro does not really tell of the affair in detail nor does he let "Your Grace" know all about him as he says he will. He is, in effect, a *histor* who chooses the reality that he observes, interpreting it in a subjective way. In choosing the adventures that he wishes to recount he gives us a partial view of reality described in realistic terms, which tends to justify the affair and his way of thinking. The narrator's subjective point of view limits the interpretation of the reality that is presented to us.

Realistic as it may seem, this work is not a true-to-life confession as some critics seem to believe. It is, in the strict sense, a fictional account presented by a fictitious writer to "Your Grace," who may, in turn, also be fictitious. The novelty of this author's use of the autobiographical form is that it is a spoken epistle written by a character/narrator to a person who is referred to in the work. Thus, the author goes well beyond the Erasmian colloquies and the autobiographical fiction of his time. The epistolary form that the author uses is more complex, and his narrator/protagonist is not wholly reliable. No doubt the author was associated with and affected by the Erasmians of the Renaissance who were looking for a new way of expressing realism to counter the idealistic literature of that time. The manner in which he portrayed the realism was quite different. Therein lies the novelty of the work.

This new form of realistic literature in which the Neoplatonic ideals of courtly life are debased coincided with Erasmian thought and its insistence on truth. It is not simply the anticlericalism found in the novel which makes it Erasmian in flavor, but also its autobiographical form, its roots in the *Colloquia,* its story of a person who is not ideal, but who observes society keenly and passes judgments on it.[6]

Modern criticism which treats *Lazarillo de Tormes* as a unified literary work that goes far beyond its precedents begins with F. Courtney Tarr's monumental article, "Literary and Artistic Unity in the *Lazarillo de Tormes.*"[7] By showing that the themes contribute to the artistic unity of the work, Tarr dispels the idea that *Lazarillo de Tormes* is simply a combination of vignettes loosely tied together. He demonstrates convincingly that the novel possesses a definite plan, an unmistakable continuity, and many elements of unity. His study was also the point of departure for the school of modern criticism which considers *Lazarillo de Tormes* to be a novel, a unified work contrived by the author.[8] The protagonist is a character who is modified and molded psychologically by his adventures and his ambience. The innocent child who has his head smashed against the bull is quite different from the vengeful child who makes his blind master smash his head against the pillar. And this child in turn is quite different from Lázaro the youth in service of the Pardoner, and Lázaro the fatalistic adult who accepts his conjugal arrangement in exchange for material benefit. *Lazarillo de Tormes* is, then, a novel with unity of structure and themes, depicting a protagonist who is developed artistically and psychologically.

Lazarillo / Lázaro: Protagonist / Narrator

Lazarillo de Tormes is a short novel which appears to be simple and overt but proves to be complex and subtle. It is not simply another fictional autobiographical narrative of its time. This novel is a mimetic narrative in the form of an autobiography, and as such its protagonist is also its narrator, and both are fictional. Because of the inventive use of the first-person form, the narrative technique itself is an aspect of fiction. It is very important to remember that the narrator is a deceptive *pícaro*. For the most part in the novel, the eyewitness narrator is a *histor* who gives an explanation of himself, and his book is a re-creation of his impression of reality. Throughout almost all of the novel, the *histor* tells the reader what he saw, did, felt, and thought.

The narrator of the novel is the adult Lázaro who relates his pseudoautobiography in letter form, while the protagonist of most of the work is Lazarillo as a boy, who is entertaining and charming in contrast to the adult Lázaro who is corrupt and hypocritical. Most readers identify with Lazarillo, the innocent, frail boy whose suffering is graphically described, especially in the first three chapters. It is for this reason that Lazarillo the boy has received most of the attention of critics and artists. Autobiographical fiction *per se* is inevitably biased, and in this novel not only does the solitary narrator present his version of the truth, which is partial and prejudiced, but he also passes off fiction as nonfiction. He justifies his deeds of the past and elicits sympathy, especially for the boy. Howard Mancing points out how the author uses description to prejudice the reader in favor of the protagonist Lazarillo.[9] There are critics who identify too much with Lazarillo the boy, and this colors their evaluation of him as a character in the work as a whole. They consider the boy to be an innocent young *pícaro* whose actions and decisions were forced upon him by a deterministic society. For some readers, the boy is good and has a heart of gold. They note this especially in his treatment of the Squire in chapter 3. Other critics take the opposite stand and think of him as a wily incorrigible thug. Woodward's interesting article on *Lazarillo de Tormes* stimulated a much needed reappraisal of the narrative technique. He rightly criticizes the overly indulgent views of Lazarillo the boy; however, he overemphasizes the link between the narrator and the boy, stressing the negative aspects of Lazarillo. Woodward calls him a "shifty

wideboy'' and a "clever young thug.''[10] It is certainly difficult not
to identify with a young protagonist who is so winning and engag-
ing; however, in order not to limit one's view of the rest of the
novel, it would be better for the reader to try to identify with the
author/narrator who, after all, presents the work in its totality.
Lazarillo the boy occupies most of the space in the narrative, but
it is Lázaro the man who plays the more important role in terms of
the novelistic technique of the author. It is Lázaro, the corrupted
adult, who supposedly has been asked by "Your Grace" to write an
account of the "affair." The written response in epistolary form is,
in effect, the book, and Lázaro, the adult and narrator, is telling the
story at the time he is town crier in the narration itself. We, as second readers, are eavesdroppers, as it were, listening to his explanation of the affair. It is important that we as readers not allow our
moral judgments, our distaste for the nonrepentant hypocritical
adult, or our sympathy for the innocent boy, to prejudice our view
of the protagonist's actions and the novel as a whole. Deyermond
points out that the reader's view of *Lazarillo de Tormes* is formed
by: (1) the events; (2) the young Lazarillo's reactions to them; (3)
the nature of Lazarillo's reflection on 1 and 2; (4) our reactions to 1,
2, and 3.[11] It is essential, then, to distinguish among various levels
of the protagonist/narrator. Lazarillo the young protagonist occupies the first five chapters of the book, and Lázaro the adult appears as protagonist in chapters 6 and 7 and reaches the "summit of
good fortune." It is Lázaro, the mature narrator of the novel and
prologue, who selects and organizes the material found therein. His
subjective point of view limits his interpretation of the reality. The
reader must keep this in mind. The actions, thought, and physical
setting are those that the supposed narrator allows us to see.

Language

In the prologue the author refers to his story as a mere trifle written in "grosero estilo" ("crude style"). What follows, however, is
really not a simple tale, and the style is anything but crude. The
author makes extensive and skillful use of figurative language and
rhetorical devices for amplification and ornamentation of words and
concepts. The stylized language and the rhetoric that he employs is

in the classical poetic tradition. Rhetoric, which was in vogue during the Renaissance, is the study of techniques used in literature and public address. These techniques include figures of speech, diction, rhythms, and structure. The embellishment of words and the skillful use of rhetoric was meant to persuade and please the audience.

The author of *Lazarillo de Tormes* was no doubt a humanist, grounded in the classical traditions, and he makes use of rhetorical devices throughout the work. Deyermond points out several elements of rhetoric.[12] *Oppositum* makes a statement and then denies its opposite so that the same statement is, in fact, made twice: "A los vecinos despertaba con el estruendo que hacía, y a mí no me dejaba dormir" ("He woke up the neighbors with the noise that he was making, and it did not let me sleep"). The basic statement *despertaba* ("woke up") and the negation of the opposite, "no me dejaba dormir" ("it did not let me sleep") is a complex device of amplification. *Pronominatio* describes the quality of a famous person: "the Blind Man compared to this one was an Alexander the Great. . . ." The stingy Blind Man is compared to Alexander the Great, noted for his generosity, thereby making the Priest of the Maqueda miserly in the extreme. *Annominatio* is a play on words from the same etymological root, or words that look and sound similar: "Y torné a jurar y perjurar que estaba libre de aquel trueco" ("I swore and swore again that I had nothing to do with the exchange"). *Traductio* involves the use of two or more words from the same root, for example, a noun and a verb. The most popular example of this in Spanish literature is Cervantes's parody of Feliciano de Silva's chivalresque romance, "la razón de la sinrazón" ("the reason of my unreason"). Deyermond points out a fine example of *traductio* in the novel: "las malas burlas que el ciego burlaba de mí" ("the bad jokes that the Blind Man played on me"). *Burla* is used as a noun and a verb. The author also makes use of *repetitio*, the repetition of a word in successive clauses: *similitudo*, similar images; *contentio*, antithetical balance; and *diminutio*, understatement.

Alberto Blecua also studies the use of rhetoric in the novel and cites some other examples.[13] *Paronomasia* is the use of words that sound almost alike but have different meanings: "¿Qué es esto Lazarillo?—Lacerado de mí, de mí—dije yo." ("What—is this Lazarillo? Lacerated me, I said to myself"). Lazarillo and *lacerado* make up the pun. *Antithesis* balances two contrasting words, ideas, or phrases: "el día que enterrábamos, yo vivía" ("the day that we would bury somebody, I would live"). *Zeugma* is a figure of speech which connects two words so that one is accurate and the other ironic: "se fue muy contento, dejándome más a mí" ("he went away happy, leaving me even more so"). These are only some of the rhetorical devices that the author uses to embellish his text.

He also uses figurative language and metaphor as an instrument of irony. His use of language, which frequently conveys both under-statement and overstatement, is used to reveal and to conceal. Deyermond cites some of the author's figurative language such as synonyms, tautology (unnecessary repetition), euphemism (the substitution of an agreeable or inoffensive expression for one that may offend or be unpleasant), polysyndeton (the repeated use of conjunctions), and others.[14]

The author varies his use of rhetorical devices from chapter to chapter.[15] In the first two he tends to personify objects or give them extraordinary qualities, thereby emphasizing their impact on Lazarillo's life. In the beginning of the first chapter the reader learns that Lázaro's father was arrested because of "ciertas sangrías" ("certain bleedings") of the miller's sacks. Later the narrator says that Lazarillo "sangraba el avariento fardel" ("used to bleed the avaricious sack"). Stealing is ennobled through language and un-derstatement, and there is a transfer of the Blind Man's stinginess to the sack. Lazarillo steals wine from the "dulce y amargo" ("sweet and bitter") wine jar. The adjectives "sweet" and "bitter" suggest the ambiguous influence that the object will have on the boy. The author uses numerous animal images, especially in chapter 1. He describes the Blind Man as a "bloodhound" when he searches for the stolen sausage by sticking his "trunk" into Lazarillo's mouth. Just before the Blind Man smashes the boy's head against the pillar he is described as a "bull" and a "goat."

Lazarillo's next master, the Priest of the Maqueda, is so miserly that, as we have seen, the Blind Man was an "Alexander the Great" compared to him. The stingy Priest eats like a "wolf" at funerals, but at home he nearly starves Lazarillo to death. In this chapter the boy seems to be losing his battle to survive, and the author uses per-sonification, especially of the Priest's old wooden chest, to describe the boy's fight with hunger. The chest is "without a heart," wounded when Lazarillo pokes holes in it, and later it becomes Lazarillo's "breadly paradise." Here the author's metaphors take on religious symbolism. The boy gets a reprieve from death when, "enlightened by the Holy Spirit," he gets the "angelic" tinker to make him a key to the chest. Lazarillo begins to steal the Priest's bread, and becomes the "serpent" who enters "paradise." Here the author uses figurative language to give the bread qualities of God. Bread is described as a *bodigo* (bread offering to the Church), and *oblada* (bread offering for the dead), and later as the "face of God." At one point the bread actually takes on the qualities of the Eucharist, and Lazarillo says that he "adores" the "face of God," not daring to "receive" it. At the end of this chapter the Priest hears a hissing noise coming from Lazarillo's breath which is passing over the key as he sleeps. Thinking that the boy is a snake the Priest smashes him on the head and knocks him out. Next he cures Lazarillo, then throws him out of the house, thereby expelling the "serpent" from paradise. The Priest is referred to as a "wolf," the very antithesis of a religious shepherd who ought to look after his flock, and he hoards his bread, the staff of life.

In chapter 3, the Squire's house is described as dark and *lóbrega* ("gloomy," "mournful"), a word which carries with it connotations of death. Later when Lazarillo sees the funeral procession and hears the wailing of the widow, the house is associated with the tomb. The Squire is described as the "Conde de Arcos," which refers to the count of Arcos, a character in Spanish ballads. He is also referred to as "Macías," a fourteenth-century troubador who was a courtly lover.

Euphemism is used to heighten the author's use of irony throughout the work. In the prologue Lázaro is writing to "Your Grace" to describe to him the *caso* ("affair"), really a *ménage à trois*. Supposedly the story will show how a man who has endured misfortune will use effort and cunning to reach a "good" port in the end. Lázaro actually does follow the example of his mother, who "determinó arrimarse a los buenos por ser uno dellos" ("decided to associate with the good people in order to become one of them"), but the ironic use of the word "good" runs throughout the novel, and it depicts material rather than moral goodness. Euphemisms are used to describe the sexual relationship that Lazarillo's mother has with Zaide, a black stable hand. She and Zaide "come to know" one another, and "continuing the conversation" they give Lazarillo a baby half-brother.

The use of the diminutive at times actually exaggerates the effect of language. In chapter 1, Lazarillo receives a tremendous blow from the wine jar, which is described as a *golpecillo* ("little blow") from the *jarillo* ("little jar"). In chapter 4 the use of the diminutive emphasizes the irony. The Monk of the Order of Mercy is described as one who is "not fond of singing in the choir and eating in the monastery." His interest lies in "secular affairs." *Mujercillas* ("little women," really, women of ill repute) call him their "relative." The most potent use of the diminutive describes Lazarillo's motive for leaving the Monk. Lazarillo as his go-between decides to quit his job with the Monk because of the latter's running around and other "cosillas que no digo" ("little things I will not mention"), which suggest the Monk's homosexual behavior. By leaving the interpretation of "little things" to the reader the author heightens the immoral behavior of the Monk. This powerful use of the diminutive leaves the reader to imagine the worst.

In chapter 6, Lázaro obtains old clothes, dresses "honorably," and thinks of himself as an "hombre de bien" ("an affluent man"); and in chapter 7 God "enlightens" him and guides him along a profitable path. He obtains a job which he euphemistically calls a Civil Service position. In plain language he is a town crier, the basest government job that exists except for executioner. Lázaro marries the mistress of the Archpriest and describes his wife as one of the "good" women of Toledo. He says that he would swear on the Sacred Host that she is as "good" a woman as any in Toledo. It is clear that he has followed his mother's example and associated with the "good" people when he says to the Archpriest: "señor . . . yo determiné de arrimarme a los buenos" ("sir . . . I decided to associate with the good people"). The neighbors begin to gossip saying, "No sé qué, y sí sé qué" ("I don't know what and I do know what"), but Lázaro silences them. Thus he is able to live the life of a cuckold and keep "peace" in his house. He is sure of his wife's "goodness," and because of this profitable arrangement he is able to say in the last sentence, with great sarcasm, that he has reached "the summit of good fortune." Figurative language depicts irony in the novel from start to finish, from the very title to the last sentence. The title *La vida de Lazarillo de Tormes y de sus fortunas y adversidades* would lead us to expect the story of a notable person; but it is really the account of an insignificant being who suffers adversities and misfortune, one who reaches the pinnacle of success or the "summit of good fortune." In a word, *Lazarillo de Tormes* is a bitter and ambiguous false success story laden with irony.

Time

In recent years there has been a considerable number of studies on the narrative technique and style of *Lazarillo de Tormes*, a vast subject which has up to this day not been exhausted. The part that the narrator plays in the work and the manner in which he arranges and relates his story are two important aspects of novelistic technique. How the author arranges and controls the time of his story provides a key to understanding his novelistic technique. There are two important studies on time in *Lazarillo de Tormes*. The first is Claudio Guillén's article, "La disposición temporal del *Lazarillo de Tormes*" ("The Arrangement of time in *Lazarillo de Tormes*"), and the other is Margit Frenk Alatorre's "Tiempo y narrador en el *Lazarillo* (episodio del ciego)" ("Time and Narrator in *Lazarillo* [The Episode of the Blind Man]").[16] Most of what follows in this section is based on these two studies. Guillén's article is not only the seminal study on the use of time in the novel, it has also served as a foundation of modern criticism dealing with the unity of the work and its technique in general. This article, like Tarr's earlier one, prepared the way for a new body of criticism on the novel. Guillén studies the chronological time in the work and demonstrates how it is subordinate to the psychological time. The main object of the narrator seems to have been to choose episodes worthy of being told and to incorporate them into the life of a character. Lázaro, the mature disillusioned adult narrator, decides how he is going to present his material. In other words, the author seems to give the narrator freedom to edit the narrative. The pseudoautobiography is by no means complete since Lázaro does not give an entire account of himself. Instead, only those episodes worthy of being told are chosen, and they are arranged, contemplated, and recounted by the adult Lázaro.

The narrator develops his selected material within a time frame, arranging the episodes of the protagonist's life, the time in which they occur, and the tempo of the episodes and chapters according to his design. Guillén says that there are three temporal planes: the time of narration, the moment in which the narrator tells, speaks, or writes; the chronological or public time of hours, days, and years; and a personal or psychological time which flows through the consciousness of a person. As Lázaro's story unfolds these three planes are reduced to two, those of the narrator (time of narration) and the protagonist (personal time). These two planes approach each other changing velocity and rhythms until the end of the novel where they converge and unite in the present tense. In the final part of the last chapter, Lázaro is simultaneously the protagonist and narrator of the novel; he is the town crier of Toledo and the cuckolded husband who relates his "affair" to "Your Grace." The present tense is used to describe to "Your Grace" his job and situation: "I live and reside in the service of God and Your Grace. I am in charge of making public announcements of wines that are to be sold in this city, and of the auctions and lost property. I also accompany those who suffer persecution under justice declaring aloud their crimes."

In chapter 1, chronological time is presented in a vague manner. Lázaro is eight years old when his father is caught stealing. The narrator says that "at that time" his father went on a crusade against the Moors. Psychological time is more significant to the narrator as he describes the moment that Lazarillo awakes from his state of innocence and begins to be a person. As Lazarillo develops as a character, personal psychological time becomes more important. The narrator tells us that Lazarillo's head hurt from the Blind Man's blow for "more than three days," making this incident implicit and intimate experience for the protagonist. From this point on, time is for the most part linked with episodes of suffering. There are three principal scenes, those of the jar, the grapes, and the sausage, which are isolated fractions of a personal time and depict the boy's apprenticeship with the Blind Man.

Chapter 2 opens with vague chronological references similar to those of chapter 1, but here the narrator introduces a new procedure. The passage of time, usually associated with the protagonist's misfortunes, begins to slow down, and the narrator begins to utilize chronological references to underline the protagonist's personal experiences and his psychological trauma. Lazarillo spends six months with the Priest of the Maqueda, and as his misfortune augments, the narrator makes more specific references to time. "After three weeks of being with him, I became so weak from hunger that I could not stand on my own two feet." Lazarillo was happy for three days when he stole bread from the chest without the Priest's noticing the theft, thereby staving off his hunger. The battle against hunger becomes more and more difficult; it endures day and night and time slows down. Finally, at the end of the chapter, the boy is unconscious for three days from a blow to his head and remains in bed for fifteen days. The slowness of time as it flows through the consciousness of the narrator accentuates Lazarillo's hunger and misery.

The use of time to increase the intensity of hunger and Lazarillo's miserable existence is developed in chapter 3. It is eight o'clock, eleven, one; the next day it is two o'clock, then four. Lazarillo's desperate plight is closely linked to time; four days pass, then three, and so on. Time is not only a framework in the chapter, it is a psychological experience. Within this slow psychological time Lazarillo lives intensely, desperately. After chapter 3, time in the novel accelerates steadily. Lazarillo's battle with hunger is not intense, and he passes through adolescence to adulthood rapidly. He spends eight days with the Monk of the Order of Mercy, four months with the Pardoner, and four years with the Chaplain. He is no longer a frail innocent boy, a victim of circumstances. His apprenticeship and his adolescence are over. Lázaro is now a man making conscious choices regarding his employment and his way of life.

Toward the end of the novel, the reader is brusquely introduced to an adult who thinks and acts for himself. Lázaro is disengaged somewhat from a deterministic environment, and he becomes a detached person, a loner who is resigned to his fate. As the author lessens the control of a deterministic environment, and as the protagonist gains control of his life, the reader tends to become less sympathetic with his plight. Lázaro has passed from the stage of innocent victim to adolescence then to adulthood, and in chapter 7, when he tells "Your Grace," "No one has heard about the affair till now," the author merges narrator with protagonist by use of the present tense. Lázaro tells his story his own way, within his own narrative framework, with his own perspective, speeding up and slowing down the passage of time as he sees fit. He uses chronological and psychological time in his way and gives an account of his life in his own style to suit his own purposes.

Using Guillén's article as a point of departure, Margit Frenk Alatorre has written an important study dealing with time and the narrator in *Lazarillo de Tormes*. She focuses her attention on the episode of the Blind Man which seems to suit her thesis best, and studies the forms and functions of time and how it relates to the narrator. In this article, time is related to the narrator and to his manipulation of space and episodes in the novel. Alatorre's study takes into account the "temps de l'histoire" ("time of the story"), otherwise known as represented or narrated time, and the "temps

de l'écriture'' (''time in writing''), known also as time of the narration.[17] Alatorre studies how both the time of the story and of the
writing operate in the novel and makes a separation of summary and
scene within the novel.[18] Summary is a generalized account of a
series of events covering an extended period and a variety of places,
and scene is the specific continuous and successive details of time,
place and action, character and dialogue. Alatorre believes that the
alternation between scenic and summary narration in the novel
determines the tempo of most of the well-developed sections of the
work, the episodes of the Blind Man, the Priest, the Squire and the
Pardoner.

The contrast between scene and summary, between showing and
telling is quite important in *Lazarillo de Tormes* when one considers
the protagonist/narrator relationship. Time is closely related to the
point of view of the single narrator, and there is one point of view
and one time of writing. The narrator can never be absent from the
text. He chooses his disguise: sometimes a little innocent boy, or an
observant adolescent, then again a cunning adult. His disguises
change, but he never disappears from the narrative. In *Lazarillo de
Tormes*, the fictitious ''I'' describes the present time which is also
fictitious, and he writes his memoirs always calculating what he
chooses to recall and relate. As he does this, he contemplates and
describes the other ''I,'' his protagonist. The life of the protagonist
develops in a past that slowly approaches the present, until past and
present merge in the last chapter. At times the narrator expresses
himself through the protagonist, at other times he acts as an in-
termediary, and at still others he addresses the reader directly. In
this pseudoautobiography, there is the perspective of the ''I'' who
lives the story and that of the ''I'' who relates it, and both these
perspectives change continually.

Lázaro the narrator appears, disappears, then reappears in the
text. He is most visible when he addresses ''Your Grace,'' especially
in the end, when he brings the narrative up to a present time. On
occasion his activities as narrator are blatantly clear: ''But I do not
want to go on and on so I will leave out a lot of things that happened
to me with this first master. . . .'' At other times he is less visible:
''as I said. . . .'' Lázaro as protagonist is a *histor* who not only in-
quires, observes, and judges but also reflects on what has gone on.
This he does in his asides, such as: ''I said to myself: 'What he says is
true. I had better keep my eyes open because I am alone and have

got to look after myself.' " Sometimes his observations are those of a boy and other times a mature adult. Speaking of his hunger in chapter 2, he says: "and so it was, because certainly at that time even the worries of the King of France would not prevent me from sleeping."[19]

According to Alatorre, the different levels of visibility of the narrator are related to the different modalities of time in the text. Of course the narrator's presence is more obvious in summary narrative than scenic. Alatorre points out examples of this distinction in chapter 1, which has two parts, an introduction and the episode of the Blind Man, making it easier to distinguish the levels of presence of the narrator and protagonist. The first unit of the chapter uses summary narrative to describe Lázaro's family background and the early stages of his youth. Some twelve years are condensed into approximately five pages.

Lazarillo's father worked in the mill for more than fifteen years, and the narrator notes, at one point in chapter 1, that the boy was eight years old. Neither reference has a very important function in the narrated time of the text. Zaide's continuing presence in the house and the "conversation" which ultimately produces a half-brother for Lazarillo suggest a passage of time.[20] For a moment time seems to stop when the narrator presents the scene of the black man and his child, and then gives the reader his reflections on the scene. Lazarillo says to himself: "How many people must there be in the world who run away from others in fright because they do not see themselves?" The narrator is blatantly present in the last paragraph of the prologue: "Your Grace has written and asked me to write and tell of the affair in detail. . . ." and in the first sentence of chapter 1: "Well, first of all Your Grace should know that they call me Lázaro de Tormes. . . ." He remains present when he describes his birth, and when he refers to Zaide as "a poor slave," "the unfortunate Zaide," and "the sad man."

The moment that the Blind Man appears, the narrator disappears behind his protagonist, and what follows is scenic narrative. There is a new manipulation of time, the narrator suppresses himself and cedes front stage to his protagonist. Lazarillo alludes to time, saying, "We were in Salamanca a few days . . . ," and here the passage of time becomes much slower than in the previous unit of chapter 1. There is also a certain type of spatial immobility. In the first part of the chapter, there is continual movement; the narrator mentions the mill, the battle at Los Gelves, his mother's moving to a house in the city, the stable of the commander of the Magdalena, and the inn of the Solana. When Lazarillo is with the Blind Man, there is no detailed description of space. The reader assumes that Lazarillo and the Blind Man wander through the streets, but the narrator does not say so directly.

The first specific scene of this chapter is that of the bull. In the narrated time, it is a brief moment. Lazarillo says that his head hurt from the blow for "three days." Except for the brief reference, "there is a stone animal there that looks like a bull . . . ," the narrator does not intervene. The protagonist is front stage, and he sets the scene and brings it to its conclusion. This is the first developed scenic narrative in the book. There is a passage of transition in which the boy and the Blind Man are on the road, which introduces the next scenic narration: "We were on the road and in just a few days he taught me thieves' slang. . . ." Summary narration will not reappear until chapter 4. Lazarillo's reflections on the Blind Man, which describe what he is like, what he does, and how he acts, stem from a cumulative knowledge.

In the episode of the jar, the narrator describes specific incidents that occur once and others that happen repeatedly. Lazarillo filches the jar over and over again, but then the narrator describes a specific episode which happens only once: "And then one day . . . I was sitting the way I used to . . . receiving those sweet drops of wine. . . ." The Blind Man at this time smashes the jar against the boy's face, breaking his teeth. The scene is described with precise details, and the protagonist's part in it makes it very immediate to the reader. The scenes of the grapes, the sausage, and the pillar are dominated by the protagonist's presence, and time seems to go slowly when they are narrated. In the episode of the pillar, the narrator emerges and comments on the prophecy of the Blind Man: "the Blind Man's prognostication proved right, and I have often thought of him since then . . . he must have had the gift of prophecy. . . . What he told me that day turned out to be true as Your Grace will hear in the future."

The narrator appears each time the narration changes from one scene to another.[21] There is one time when, during the episode of the wine jar, the narrator appears and the scene does not change. In this passage, which is the most dramatic part of the episode, the narrator refers to Lázaro as protagonist using the third person. He describes how the Blind Man took revenge: "with all his strength he lifted the jar, which had been the source of pleasure and was now to be the instrument of pain, and from high over his head he let it fall straight on my mouth, as I am telling you, helped with all the strength he could muster. *Poor Lázaro* was not expecting this; in fact, *he* was relaxed and enjoying *himself* as before. I really felt as if the roof and everything on it had fallen on top of me" (my italics). When the voice of the narrator enters, he creates a distance between himself and the protagonist.

The omniscient narrator appears in this episode and describes to the reader how the Blind Man felt the jar and discovered the hole in it, a fact that the unsuspecting protagonist is unaware of. The Blind Man hides this discovery from the boy, and only the omniscient narrator knows the precise moment that the Blind Man will take his vengeance. In preparation for the Blind Man's vengeance, the author denotes the limitations of the protagonist, relating not only what he sees but also what he thinks and surmises. Lazarillo is sucking the wine out with the straw and says of the Blind Man: "But the traitor was so sharp that *I think* he heard me and from then on changed his plan . . ." (my italics). After stealing the sausage, he says that the Blind Man "seized me by the head, and bent down to smell me. He *must have* got the scent like a bloodhound. . ." (my italics). When Lázaro returns with the wine, the omniscient narrator says that the Blind Man was ready to take a bite of the turnip, because he "had not felt it and found out . . . that it was not a sausage." Lazarillo is not there and does not know this to be a fact. Only the omniscient narrator can give the reader this information. The author is very deliberate and knows exactly what he is doing when he has the narrator emerge, disappear, observe, and acknowledge his limitations. Infrequently, the narrator acknowledges his limitations and the omniscient narrator appears. The author's narrator as *histor* does not have the absolute power that the omniscient narrator has.

The main purpose of the author seems to have been to incorporate incidents in the life of his protagonist. The past is suppressed by and converges with the present tense in the last chapter when the town crier refers to his story in the present.[22] From time to time, the mature disillusioned narrator, Lázaro, appears and reflects on the past, but for the most part the reader is present with the *histor* as episodes transpire. The scenic narration gives an illusion of immediate reality with the mediation of the narrator, as if the reader also were an eyewitness to the scene. However, there are also subtle interventions of the narrator, which place scenes before the eyes of the reader who is unaware of their having taken place.

The main object of the narrator seems to have been to choose episodes worthy of being retold and incorporating them into the existence of the character. The mature and disillusioned adult narrator decides how he is going to present his material. In other words, the author gives the narrator the freedom to edit the narrated material. Thus, only those episodes worthy of being told are chosen, and they are situated, contemplated, and edited by the adult Lázaro. The three temporal planes of time approach one another with a variety of changing tempos and rhythms until, at the end of the novel, Lázaro is simultaneously the protagonist and narrator of the novel. He is town crier of Toledo and a complacent cuckold, and he uses the present tense to describe his position. He says of his Civil Service job: "I still have it *today* . . ." (my italics). The narrator *is* the protagonist, and the form of the novel follows a life remembered and interpreted, the story of a protagonist who projects himself backwards into time—one who sees himself from within and without. He is a careful narrator who is always in control, and the best way to see this is to study the various aspects of time and how he manipulates them. The narration is subordinated to a self-definition from the past to the present.

Chapter Seven
Conclusion

Lazarillo de Tormes is a literary work that is universal in scope. The numerous editions, translations, and scholarly studies that have been done attest to the premier position that it holds in the ranks of the picaresque genre, Spain's original contribution to the development of the modern novel. Readers over the ages have been intrigued by the problems of the absence of a *princeps* edition and by the anonymity of the author, as well as by the book's content, structure, and style.

The author's sophisticated style, which incorporates several literary and cultural traditions, shows him to be an eclectic humanist who adapted his material well. However, he was first and foremost a creator. He had no real model from which to learn. Instead, with his innovative technique and style he created a model for the picaresque genre, a progenitor of the modern novel.

Judging by the three separate editions that appeared in Burgos, Alcalá, and Antwerp in 1554, followed quickly by others published both in and out of Spain, one can conclude that the book was popular from the beginning. Many scholars have searched for a *princeps* edition to no avail. Although there is mention of editions earlier than those published in 1554, to this date none has been found. The anonymity of such a well written and popular novel has also drawn the attention of many readers.

The polemic surrounding the authorship started soon after the book's first known publication date, and continues to thrive. Since scholars have not been able to identify *who* the author was, they have tried to identify *what* he was. Using the text, its themes, its use of language, and its style they have speculated on his ideological and religious beliefs. Some hold the opinion that it would have been imprudent for the author to reveal himself, and that the book's autobiographical style and its anonymity are inextricable. In spite of the considerable investigation into the authorship of the novel, its anonymity and the reasons for it remain a mystery, and the author, if he wished to remain anonymous, has succeeded.

The most striking formal aspect of the work is its innovative autobiographical style, the most salient stylistic feature its irony which pervades the book. In the prologue the author, who evidently could afford to be modest, refers to his book as a "nonada" ("trifle"), written in "grosero estilo" ("crude style"). His work is anything but a simple story and his style anything but crude; as such the book can be read on at least two levels. He goes on to say that casual readers will find things in it that will please them, but those who penetrate deeply into the text will be delighted by it. Penetrating readers and critics from various continents have not only been delighted by the work, they have been intrigued and puzzled over the years by its ironic narrative and its cunning narrator.

Lázaro, as an act of supposed obedience, writes a controlled and contrived account of his life, its adversities, and its fortunes. Presumably he has been asked by "Your Grace" to explain the "affair" in detail. Lázaro's relation reveals, withholds, and obfuscates information, showing him to be an adroit and devious narrator who is always in control of his text. He chooses the reality that he observes as an eyewitness character, and recounts his story by interpreting it as he sees fit. He commands the constant attention of the reader as he sketches his career from innocent childhood to cynical adulthood in a witty and persuasive manner.

The prologue promises the complete story of an individual who has overcome adversity and succeeded in reaching a "good port," but what actually follows is a partial account of a pseudosuccess story, a story of a debased character who surrenders himself to a corrupt world. As Lázaro's relation of his past approaches the present time of narration, the depravity of the protagonist becomes more and more evident. The narrator's explanation of the "affair" and the partial account of his life offer circumstantial evidence which both implicates him in and exonerates him from the corrupt society in which he lives and thrives. The combination of implication and exoneration produces an ironic narrative in which appearances are almost always deceiving. Lázaro portrays himself as corrupt, but no better, no worse than those who surround him.[1] From the prologue to the final chapter Lázaro seems to be putting things in a proper context—his own of course. After reading the novel and returning to the prologue the reader realizes that not only has Lázaro explained very little about the "affair," he has also justified it to a certain extent by emphasizing the deterministic events that lead up to it. Thus has he put things in their proper perspective.

Lázaro has redefined the project given to him by "Your Grace," and his plan, to give an account of himself starting "at the beginning, not the middle" was accepted by the reader *a priori* in the prologue. Through a skillful use of cynical determinism combined with free will, the narrator has given us his account of the strange story of one Lázaro González Pérez, lowly citizen of Renaissance Spain, who with great effort and cunning combatted adverse fortune and arrived at a "good" port.

Notes and References

Chapter One

1. Frank Wadleigh Chandler, *Romances of Roguery* (New York, 1961), pp. 45–46.

2. Kay Seymour House, *Cooper's Americans* (Columbus: Ohio State University Press, 1965), p. 307. In his talk, "Picaresque Paradigms," Midwest Modern Language Association Meeting, Indianapolis, 10 November, 1979, Dennis Lynch treated four distinct types of protagonists in picaresque novels, and unfortunately considered Don Quixote to be a "picaresque saint." See A. Owen Aldridge, "Fenimore Cooper and the Picaresque Tradition," *Nineteenth Century Fiction* 17 (1972): 283–92, which includes the views of American literary scholars on the picaresque.

3. Walter Ernest Allen, *The English Novel* (London: Phoenix, 1954), p. 30. Some others who apply the term broadly are Robert Alter, *Rogue's Progress: Studies in the Picaresque Novel* (Cambridge, Mass., 1964); R. W. B. Lewis, *The Picaresque Saint* (Philadelphia: J. B. Lippincott, 1959); and D. M. Dooley, "Some Uses and Mutations of the Picaresque," *Dalhousie Review* 37 (1957–58): 363–77.

4. Harold Child, "The Age of Johnson," in *Cambridge History of English Literature,* ed. A. W. Ward and A. R. Waller (New York: G. P. Putnam's Sons, 1913), 10:47.

5. There are some good studies on British and American novels and how they relate to the picaresque. See for example G. S. Rousseau, "Smollett and the Picaresque: Some Questions about a Label," *Studies in Burke and His Time* 12 (1971): 1886–1904; Nicholas Spadaccini, "Daniel Defoe and the Spanish Picaresque Tradition: The Case of *Moll Flanders,*" *Ideologies and Literatures* 2 (1978): 10–26. With regard to the confusion of the term picaresque, W. H. Frohock questions the use of the term and believes that when it is applied to Spanish literature there is an adequate definition of it. In "The Idea of the Picaresque," *Yearbook of General and Comparative Literature* 16 (1967), his solution is "to use the term only when we must but with the realization that when we use it we count on being misunderstood" (p. 52). In his article, "The Failing Center: Recent Fiction and the Picaresque Tradition," *Novel* 3 (1960), Frohock criticizes the loose use of the term saying: "For every novelist to write a new novel, there is at least one critic waiting to find something picaresque in it" (p. 64).

6. Alter, *Rogue's Progress*, p. 9.

7. Alexander A. Parker, *Literature and the Delinquent: The Picaresque Novel in Spain and Europe 1599-1753* (Edinburgh: Edinburgh University Press, 1967), p. 28.

8. Stuart Miller, *The Picaresque Novel* (Cleveland, 1967).

9. W. M. Frohock, "The Idea of the Picaresque," *Yearbook of General and Comparative Literature* 16 (1967): 43-52.

10. Daniel Eisenberg, "Does the Picaresque Novel Exist?" paper presented at the Kentucky Foreign Language Conference, in Lexington, Kentucky, 23 April 1976.

11. Claudio Guillén, "Toward a Definition of the Picaresque," in *Literature as System: Essays Toward the Theory of Literary History* (Princeton, N.J., 1971), pp. 71-106, which first appeared in *Proceedings of the International Comparative Literature Association*, ed. W. A. P. Smit (The Hague: Mouton & Co.). See also his "Genre and Countergenre: The Discovery of the Picaresque," pp. 135-58.

12. Guillén, *Literature as System*, p. 71.

13. Ibid., pp. 79-84.

14. See ibid., p. 73.

15. Ulrich Wicks, "Pícaro Picaresque: The Picaresque in Literary Scholarship," *Genre* 5 (1972): 153-92, which includes a bibliography of studies on the picaresque; "The Nature of Picaresque Narrative: A Modal Approach," *PMLA* 89 (1974): 240-49; "Onlyman," *Mosaic* 8, no. 3 (1975): 21-47; "The Romance of the Picaresque," *Genre* 11 (1978): 29-44.

16. Fernando Lázaro Carreter, "'Para una revisión del concepto 'Novela Picaresca,' '" in *"Lazarillo de Tormes" en la picaresca* (Barcelona, 1972), pp. 195-229.

17. Francisco Rico, *La novela picaresca y el punto de vista* (Barcelona, 1970), includes some excellent insights into specific picaresque novels; Christine J. Whitbourne, *Knaves and Swindlers* (Oxford, 1974); Harry Sieber, *The Picaresque* (London, 1977); Richard Bjornson, *The Picaresque Hero in European Fiction* (Madison, 1977) offers a good comprehensive survey of picaresque novels placing them in a social context; Peter N. Dunn, *The Spanish Picaresque Novel* (Boston, 1979). Other notable studies on the picaresque are Manuel Criado de Val, ed., *La picaresca: orígenes, textos y estructuras* (Madrid, 1979), which contains helpful material on the picaresque as well as on specific novels; Howard Mancing, "The Picaresque Novel: A Protean Form"; and Ulrich Wicks, "Narrative Distance" in Picaresque Fiction," *College Literature* 6 (1979): 165-81 and 182-204 respectively. This volume includes articles on the picaresque in American and British literature and a bibliographic essay; other useful studies are Alexander Blackburn, *The Myth of the Pícaro: Continuity and Transformation of the Picaresque Novel 1554-1954* (Chapel Hill, 1979);

Alan Francis, *Picaresca, decadencia, historia* (Madrid, 1978); Maurice Molho, *Romans picaresques espagnols* (Paris, 1968); Frederick Monteser, *The Picaresque Element in Western Literature* (University: University of Alabama Press, 1975); Julio Rodríguez-Luis, "Pícaras: The Modal Approach to the Picaresque," *Comparative Literature* 31 (1979): 32–46; Jenaro Talens, *Novela picaresca y práctica de la transgresión* (Madrid: Júcar, 1975); Gustavo A. Alfaro, *La estructura de la novela picaresca* (Bogotá, 1977).

18. For a useful study on *mythos,* mimetic fiction, the empirical mode, and the use of *histor,* see Robert Scholes and Robert Kellogg, *The Nature of Narrative* (London: Oxford University Press, 1975), pp. 3–16, 240–66.

19. For a comparison of the concept of reality found in the picaresque and Cervantes's *Novelas ejemplares,* see Carlos Blanco Aguinaga, "Cervantes y la picaresca. Notas sobre dos tipos de realismo," *Nueva revista de filología hispánica* 11 (1947): 313–46.

20. For a discussion of the *desengaño* theme, see Stephen Gilman, *Symposium* 1 (1946): 82–107, and Otis Green, *Spain and the Western Tradition* (Madison: University of Wisconsin Press, 1966), 4: 43–76.

21. Parker, *Literature and the Delinquent,* p. 22. Enrique Moreno Báez, in his *Lección y sentido de Guzmán de Alfarache* (Madrid: C.S.I.C., 1948), points out how the religious ends of the Counter-Reformation of Spain reflect the theological preoccupations of the time. He was the first to argue convincingly that certain theological principles such as Original Sin, Salvation, and Free Will are germane to the *Guzmán.*

Chapter Two

1. There is a facsimile edition of the three texts edited by Antonio Pérez Gómez (Cieza: La fonte que mana y corre, 1959), with an introduction by Enrique Moreno Báez. R. O. Jones has also edited the three separate editions (Manchester: Manchester University Press, 1963).

2. Jacques Charles Brunet, *Manuel de libraire et de l'amateur des livres* (Paris: Libraire de Fermin-Didot, 1880), 2: 270.

3. Adolfo Bonilla y San Martín, in the introduction to his edition of *La vida de Lazarillo de Tormes* (Madrid, 1915), p. xiv, believes that the Duque de T'Serclaes was the first owner of this edition which later was obtained by Marqués de Jerez de los Caballeros. The Marqués's library was acquired first by A. M. Huntington and later by the Hispanic Society of America. There is, however, no mention of this edition in Clara Louise Penny's *List of Books printed before 1601 in the Library of The Hispanic Society of America* (New York: Hispanic Society of America, 1929), and there is not much likelihood that it really exists.

4. Louis Viardot, *Études sur l'histoire des institutions, de la littérature, du théâtre et des beaux-arts en Espagne* (Paris: Paulin, 1835).

5. Aristide Rumeau, "Notes au *Lazarillo* (Des editions d'Anvers, 1554–1555, à celles de Milan, 1587–1615,)" *Bulletin Hispanique* 66 (1964): 271–93; "Notes sur les 'Lazarillo' editions d'Anvers, 1553 in 16," *Bulletin Hispanique* 66 (1964): 57–64.

6. Alfred Paul Morel-Fatio, *Études sur l'Espagne* (Paris: Bouillon, 1890), pp. 111–66.

7. Alberto Blecua studies with care the interpolations of the Alcalá text in the introduction of his edition of *Lazarillo de Tormes* (Madrid, 1974), pp. 57–59, and is convinced that they are not by the original author.

8. Alfredo Cavaliere, introduction to his edition of *Lazarillo de Tormes* (Naples, 1955); José Caso González, introduction to his edition of *Lazarillo de Tormes* (Madrid, 1967); Francisco Rico, "En torno al texto crítico de *Lazarillo de Tormes*," *Hispanic Review* 38 (1970): 405–19, and the introduction to his edition of *Lazarillo de Tormes* (Barcelona, 1967), pp. ix–xv; and Alberto Blecua, introduction to his edition of *Lazarillo de Tormes* (Madrid, 1974), pp. 7–15, 48–70.

9. See his "En torno al texto crítico," pp. 405–19, and *Lazarillo*, pp. ix–xv.

10. José Caso González, "La primera edición del *Lazarillo de Tormes* y su relación con los textos de 1554," in *Studia Hispanica in Honorem R. Lapesa*, (Madrid: Gredos, 1972), 1: 189–206.

11. Blecua, *Lazarillo*, p. 56.

12. Among those who opt for this date are Cavaliere, *Lazarillo*, pp. 9–13; Alberto del Monte, *Itinerario de la novela picaresca española* (Barcelona, 1971), pp. 17–18; Manuel J. Asensio, "La intención religiosa de *Lazarillo de Tormes*," *Hispanic Review* 26 (1959): 78–83; Ricapito, *Lazarillo de Tormes* (Madrid: Cátedra, 1976), pp. 16–17.

13. For a résumé of the problems regarding these dates see Asensio, "La intención," p. 80.

14. Ibid. p. 79, and Asensio, "Más sobre el *Lazarillo de Tormes*," *Hispanic Review* 28 (1960): 250.

15. Ricapito, *Lazarillo*, p. 22.

16. Some critics calculate his age to be nine years old (*Itinerario*, p. 18), which shows the inaneness of looking for an exact chronology in the novel.

17. Asensio, "La intención," pp. 78–102.

18. Blecua, *Lazarillo*, p. 15.

Chapter Three

1. A. Rumeau, "Notes au 'Lazarillo,' " pp. 272–93.

2. Guillén, *Literature as System*, pp. 139–40, also says that the Flemish edition was the basis for the Milan reprints of 1587 and 1597, and for the first English and French translations.

3. For a discussion on the modifications, see Rico, *Lazarillo*, p. lxxiii; Hans Gerd Rötzer *Picaro-Landstortzer-Simplicius* (Darmstadt: Wissenschaftliche Buchgesellschaft, 1972), pp. 29–31, and Bataillon, *Novedad*, pp. 72–73.

4. There were later editions in 1722, 1728, 1746 in Madrid, and in 1769 in Valencia and Barcelona.

5. For studies on this novel, see Bjornson, *Picaresque Hero*, pp. 98–101; Robert S. Rudder, "La segunda parte de *Lazarillo de Tormes*: La originalidad de Juan de Luna," *Estudios filológicos*, 6 (1970): 97–112; Jean-Marc Pelorson and Hélène Simon, "Une mise au point sur *l'Arte Breve* de Juan de Luna," *Bulletin hispanique* 71 (1969): 218–30; Joseph L. Laurenti, *Vida de Lazarillo de Tormes: Estudio crítico de La segunda parte de Juan de Luna* (Mexico City: Studium, 1965); and Bataillon, *Novedad*, chap. 6; Marina Scordilis Brownlee, "Generic Subversion: The Two Continuations of *Lazarillo de Tormes*," *Philological Quarterly* 61 (1982): 317–25.

6. Laurenti in his *Vida* and Angel Valbuena Prat in his *La novela picaresca* (Madrid: Aguilar, 1964) criticize Luna for distorting the original.

7. See Horst Baader, "Lazarillos Weg zur Eindeutigkeit oder Juan de Luna als Leser und Interpret desanonymen *Lazarillo de Tormes*," in *Interpretation und Vergleich: Festschrift für Walter Pabst*, ed. Eberhard Leube Schrader (Berlin: Erich Schmidt, 1972), pp. 11–33.

8. This is reprinted in *Lazarillos raros*, ed. Richard Zwez (Valencia: Albatrós, 1972), pp. 93–116.

9. Bjornson, *Picaresque Hero*, p. 67; for a study of the early editions, see Guillén, *Literature as System*, pp. 137–46.

10. Benito Brancaforte and Charlotte Brancaforte, eds. *La primera traducción del "Lazarillo de Tormes" por Giulio Strozzi* (Ravenna, 1977). This is a translation of the Antwerp edition of 1554 and the anonymous second part of 1555. The editors believe that Strozzi identifies himself by use of an anagrammatic pseudonym.

11. This is included in the 1616 edition published in Paris by Adrian Tiffaine.

12. See Bjornson, *Picaresque Hero*, pp. 70–71, 87–88, 97–99, 127–28; Guillén, *Literature as System*, pp. 136–48; Zwez, *Lazarillos raros*.

Chapter Four

1. *Historia de la Orden de San Gerónimo*, in *Nueva biblioteca de autores españoles* 12 (1909): 145.

2. Morel-Fatio, *La Vie de Lazarillo de Tormes*, p. xvi; Marcel Bataillon, *La Vie de Lazarillo de Tormes* (Paris, 1958), pp. 14–16; Manuel García Blanco, *La Lengua española en la época de Carlos V* (Madrid: Escelicer, 1967), pp. 21 ff.

3. Manuel J. Asensio, "Más sobre *el Lazarillo,*" *Hispanic Review* 28 (1961): 245; Joseph H. Silverman, *Romance Philology* 15 (1961): 90.

4. *Catalogus Clarorum Hispaniae Scriptorum* (Mainz: B. Lippius, 1607), p. 44.

5. Published under the pseudonym Andreus Peregrinus, *Hispaniae Bibliotheca* (Frankfort, 1608), p. 543.

6. "Junta de Libros" Ms. Biblioteca Nacional de Madrid, f. 23, p. 136; see also Nicolás Antonio, *Bibliotheca Hispana Nova* (Madrid: J. de Ibarra, 1783), p. 291.

7. See Joseph P. Ricapito, *Bibliografía razonada y anotada de las obras maestras de la novela picaresca* (Madrid, 1976); Angel González Palencia, "Leyendo el *Lazarillo de Tormes,*" in *Del Lazarillo a Quevedo* (Madrid: C.S.I.C. 1946), pp. 22–30; Angel González Palencia and Eugenio Mele, *Vida y obras de don Diego Hurtado de Mendoza* (Madrid: E. Maestre, 1943), 3: 205–22; Erika Spivakovsky, "Valdés o Mendoza?" *Hispanófila* 12 (1961): 15–23; "The *Lazarillo de Tormes* and Mendoza," *Symposium* 15 (1961): 271–85; and her "New arguments in favor of Mendoza's Authorship of the *Lazarillo de Tormes,*" *Symposium* 25 (1970): 67–80; Fred Abrams, "Hurtado de Mendoza's Concealed Signatures in the *Lazarillo de Tormes,*" *Romance Notes* 15 (1974): 341–45.

8. Fonger de Haan, *An Outline of the History of the Novela Picaresca in Spain* (The Hague, 1903), p. 3; Fred Abrams, "¿Fue Lope de Rueda el autor del *Lazarillo de Tormes?*" *Hispania* 47 (1946): 258–67.

9. Asensio begs the question in *Sebastián de Horozco: noticias y obras inéditas de este autor dramático desconocido* (Seville: D. J. M. Geofrin, 1867); Julio Cejador ·y Frauca, *Cancionero de Sebastián de Horozco* (Seville: 1876), p. 157, and his introduction to *La vida de Lazarillo de Tormes* (Madrid, 1914), p. 57; F. Márquez Villanueva, "Sebastián de Horozco y el *Lazarillo de Tormes,*" *Revista de filología hispánica* 41 (1957): 253–339.

10. María Rosa Lida de Malkiel, "La función del cuento popular en el *Lazarillo de Tormes*" in *Actas del primer congreso internacional de hispanistas,* ed. Frank Pierce and Cyril A. Jones (Oxford: Dolphin, 1964), p. 654, n. 4.

11. See Alfred Morel-Fatio's introduction to *Lazarillo de Tormes* (Paris, 1886), and his *Études sur l'Espagne,* (Paris, F. Vieweg, 1888), p. 156.

12. Marcel Bataillon, *Erasmo y España,* trans. Antonio Alatorre (Mexico City: Fondo de cultura económica, 1950), p. 610.

13. Manuel J. Asensio, "La intención religiosa de *Lazarillo de Tormes* y Juan de Valdés," *Hispanic Review* 27 (1959): 73–102; Joseph P. Ricapito in his introduction to *Lazarillo de Tormes* (Madrid, 1976), pp. 44–55; See also Francisco Rico's introduction to the novel (1976), p. 21.

14. The most complete arguments in favor of the author's being a con-

vert are found in Américo Castro's *Hacia Cervantes* (Madrid, 1957), pp. 19–31.

15. F. Márquez Villanueva, in "La actitud espiritual del *Lazarillo de Tormes*," in *Espiritualidad y literatura en el siglo XVI* (Madrid: Alfaguara, 1968), pp. 115 ff., insists on Toledo as the location of the novel, a center of persecutions against New Christians and location of the polemic against the Hapsburgs. See also del Monte, *Itinerario de la novela picaresca*, p. 27, n. 102; Enrique Tierno Galván, "¿Es el *Lazarillo* un libro comunero?" in *Boletín informativo del seminario de derecho político*, nos. 20–23 (Universidad de Salamanca, 1958), 217 ff.

16. Among those who find merit in Castro's views are Bataillon, *Erasmo y España*, p. 612, n. 5; Francisco Lázaro Carreter, "Construcción y sentido del *Lazarillo de Tormes*," *Ábaco* 1 (1969): 130; Claudio Guillén in his introduction to *Lazarillo de Tormes* (New York, 1966), pp. 33–34.

17. Guillén, *Lazarillo*, p. 33.

18. Northrup Frye, *The Anatomy of Criticism* (Princeton: Princeton University Press, 1971), pp. 223–24.

19. Castro, *Hacia Cervantes*, p. 157.

20. Castro, *Aspectos del vivir hispánico*, p. 45.

21. Morel-Fatio, "La intención religiosa del *Lazarillo de Tormes* y Juan de Valdés," *Hispanic Review* 27 (1959): 78–102; "Más sobre el *Lazarillo de Tormes*," *Historical Review* 28 (1960): 245–50. Both Anson Piper, "The Breadly Paradise of *Lazarillo de Tormes*," *Hispania* 44 (1961): 269–70, and Otis H. Green, *Spain and the Western Tradition*, (Madison: University of Wisconsin Press, 1965), 3: 149–50, accept Asensio's theory; Bataillon rejects it (*Erasmo y España*, p. 610).

22. Alberto del Monte believes that Asensio's arguments are easily refuted by Bataillon (in *Erasmo y España*, p. 610), *Itinerario de la novela picaresca*, p. 28. However, Asensio's arguments have been convincing enough for some critics to conclude that the author was an Erasmian.

23. See Ricapito, *Lazarillo*, pp. 41–42, 44–51; for further thoughts on whether or not the author was Erasmian see E. Spivakovsky, "¿Valdés o Mendoza?," pp. 15–23, and her "The *Lazarillo de Tormes* and Mendoza," *Symposium* 25 (1961): 171–85; O. Crouch, "El autor del *Lazarillo de Tormes* sobre [sic] una reciente tesis," *Hispanófila* 19 (1963): 11–23.

24. Rico, Introduction to *Lazarillo de Tormes* pp. lix–lx.

25. Robert Fiore, "*Lazarillo de Tormes*: estructura narrativa de una novela picaresca," in *La picaresca: orígenes, textos y estructuras*, ed. Manuel Criado de Val (Madrid, 1979), p. 365.

26. Ricapito, *Lazarillo*, p. 42.

27. Asensio, "Intención religiosa," pp. 101–2; see also Bataillon, *Erasmo y España*, pp. 230–36.

Chapter Five

1. For example, *Les fortunes et adversitez du feu noble homme Jehan Regnier* by Jehan Regnier (Geneva: Paul Lacroix, 1867).

2. For a study on the resemblance of the name Lazarus and similar Spanish words that denote misery, see Yakov Malkiel, "La familia léxica, lazerar, las(d)rar, laceria," *Nueva revista de filología hispánica* 6 (1952): 209–76.

3. Stephen Gilman studies the notion of Lázaro's spiritual death in "The Death of Lazarillo de Tormes," *PMLA* 81 (1966): 149–66.

4. The title does not mean Lazarillo of the River Tormes; that would have been written with the definite article "*del* Tormes." "De Tormes," as the narrator later explains, means that he was born right on the river.

5. Frank Durand believes that what started as an account for one man may well have reached more ambitious proportions. See "The Author and Lázaro: Levels of Comic Meaning," *Bulletin of Hispanic Studies* 45 (1968): 88–101.

6. My guess is that the word "trifle" is used by an author who, because of high social status, could afford to be modest.

7. All quotations in Spanish are taken from Joseph V. Ricapito's well-annotated and readily available edition (Madrid, 1976), pp. 95–97.

8. Bruce W. Wardropper studies the ironic use of the word *bueno* and the inverted value system of the novel, in "El trastorno de la moral en el *Lazarillo*," *Nueva revista de filología hispánica* 15 (1961): 441–47.

9. C.P. Wagner noted the difference between the epigraphs and the chapters in his introduction, p. xxii; see also F. Courtney Tarr, "Literary and Artistic Unity in the *Lazarillo de Tormes*," *PMLA* 42 (1927): 404–21. Francisco Rico maintains that this epigraph fulfilled the author's intention, *Lazarillo*, p. xiv.

10. Guillén, *Lazarillo de Tormes*, pp. 28, 136; Gilman, "Death of Lazarillo," p. 161; Anthony T. Perry, "Biblical Symbolism in the *Lazarillo de Tormes*," *Studies in Philology* 67 (1970): 139–46; and Víctor de la Concha, "La intención religiosa del Lazarillo," *Revista de filología española* 55 (1972): 243–77.

11. Julio Cejador y Frauca was one of the first to notice the double biblical origin of the name Lazarus in his introduction to *Lazarillo de Tormes* (Madrid, 1941), p. 17. Others followed: Guillén, *Lazarillo*, pp. 27–28, 136; A. D. Deyermond, *Lazarillo de Tormes: A Critical Guide* (London, 1975), pp. 27–30; Bruce W. Wardropper, "The Strange Case of Lázaro González Pérez," *Modern Language Notes*, 92 (1977): 201–12.

12. "And he confessed and denied not; but confessed, I am not the Christ" (John 1:20).

13. "Blessed are they which are persecuted for righteousness' sake: for theirs is the Kingdom of Heaven" (Matthew 5:10). Gilman stresses the

combination of skepticism, black humor, and irony in this sentence, in "Castilian Jest and Earnest," in *Studia Hispanica in Honorem R. Lapesa* (Madrid: Gredos, 1973), 1: 257–65; see also Perry, pp. 139–46.

14. Bruce W. Wardropper, "El trastorno de la moral en el *Lazarillo,*" *Nueva revista de filología hispánica* 15 (1961): 442; see also Tarr, "Literary and Artistic Unity," p. 418.

15. In the last sentence of the book, the narrator describes his pseudo-success by saying "pues en este tiempo estaba en mi prosperidad y en la cumbre de toda buena fortuna" ("at that time I was prosperous and at the height of good fortune").

16. Besides the thirteen asides there are eight occurrences of unnoted speech which serve a different function. Douglas M. Carey studies and classifies the asides in "Asides and Interiority in *Lazarillo de Tormes:* A Study in Psychological Realism," *Studies in Philology* 66 (1969): 119–34. A. Marasso notes that the asides are like those found in classical drama, "La elaboración del *Lazarillo de Tormes,*" in *Estudios de la literatura castellana* (Buenos Aires: Kapelusz, 1955), p. 165.

17. Guillén, *Lazarillo,* p. 20.

18. Harry Sieber points out the significance of the verb *veo* here, in *Language and Society in "La vida de Lazarillo de Tormes"* (Baltimore, 1978), p. 14.

19. Frank Durand, "The Author and Lázaro: Levels of Comic Meaning," *Bulletin of Hispanic Studies* 45 (1968): 95. Durand includes some excellent perceptions and well-reasoned conclusions in his articles. Howard Mancing observes rightly that through the intimacy of autobiographical style the author prejudices the reader in favor of the protagonist, in "The Deceptiveness of *Lazarillo de Tormes,*" *PMLA* 90 (1975): 426–32.

20. Tarr, "Literary and Artistic Unity," p. 105, was the first to point out the progressive theme of hunger and how it contributed to the artistic unity of the novel.

21. Bataillon, *Erasmo,* p. 610; Asensio, "Intención," p. 100.

22. Castro, *Hacia Cervantes,* p. 154; Ricapito, *Lazarillo de Tormes,* pp. 131–33, 137, discusses critical views of Erasmian influence, including Valbuena's. For a well annotated list of studies dealing with the religious, philosophical, and moral views of the author, see his *Bibliografía razonada y anotada de las obras maestras de la picaresca española* (Madrid, 1980), pp. 363–72.

23. Del Monte, *Itinerario de la novela picaresca española,* p. 45.

24. Lázaro Carreter, *"Lazarillo,"* p. 124. Tarr, "Literary and Artistic Unity", p. 65, recognized this chapter as an original narrative creation of no mean artistic ability.

25. Deyermond, *Lazarillo,* p. 65.

26. Animal images abound in the book, for example, the Blind Man is

compared to a bloodhound, and a billy goat, and his nose to a trunk. Here, as Deyermond observes, *Lazarillo,* pp. 68–69, the Priest, who by traditional Christian metaphor is a shepherd of his flock, is compared to a wolf who devours possessions of his flock.

27. It is interesting to note that Tarr, in 1927, noticed what he calls unusual metaphors: "cara de Dios" ("face of God"), "paraíso panal" ("breadly paradise"), and "angélico calderero" ("angelic tinker") in his seminal study, "Literary and Artistic Unity," p. 408, n. 12. Other helpful studies also treat this chapter: Alter, in *Rogue's Progress,* pp. 2–10, claims that Lazarillo's world is ordered by God and that the narrator can therefore explain the presence of the "angelic tinker" as an act of God; Asensio studies the religious attitudes and situation of the time, and believes that treatment of the Holy Eucharist reveals contact with the Illuminist thought of that period, "La intención religiosa del *Lazarillo de Tormes* y Juan de Valdés," *Hispanic Review* 26 (1959): 78–102; Anson C. Piper, in "The Breadly Paradise of Lazarillo de Tormes," *Hispania* 44 (1961): 269–71, sees a symbolic significance in Lazarillo's battle with the chest and identifies the chest with the Church's final victory over heresy; Juan Ter-lingen does not believe that the "face of God" is an irreverent reference to the Eucharist "Cara de Dios," in *Studia Philologica: Homenaje ofrecido a Dámaso Alonso* (Madrid: Gredos, 1963) 3:463–78; Ricapito emphasizes convincingly the religious and moral aspect of the "face of God," "Cara de Dios: Ensayo de rectificación," *Bulletin of Hispanic Studies* 50 (1973): 142–46; see also Jack Weiner, "La lucha de Lazarillo de Tormes por el ar-ca," in *Actas del tercer congreso internacional de hispanistas* (Mexico City, 1969), pp. 93–134 and his "El ciego y las dos hambres de Lázaro de Tormes," in *Literatura española clásica* (Valparaiso, Chile: Universidad Católica de Valparaiso, 1971), 5: 3–36, esp. pp. 18–25; and Walter Holz-inger, "The Breadly Paradise Revisited: *Lazarillo de Tormes, segundo tratado,*" *Revista hispánica moderna,* p. 37.

28. Lázaro Carreter, *Lazarillo,* p. 125–27, sees the tinker and the boy in folkloric terms. The tinker serves the function as a helper for the hero to escape misfortune.

29. Guillén, introduction to *Lazarillo,* p. 18.

30. Asensio, Márquez Villanueva, Piper, and others see heterodoxy here. For a review of this subject see Víctor de la Concha, "La intención religiosa del *Lazarillo,*" *Revista de filología española* 55 (1972): 259–68. Rico, *Lazarillo,* pp. lxii–ix; and Ricapito, *Lazarillo,* pp. 131–37, and his *Bibliografía,* pp. 349–50, 364–72, are exponents of Erasmian influences.

31. "Enlightened by I don't know whom," in the expurgated edition of 1573.

32. Some critics have interpreted the reference to the Holy Eucharist as irreverent: Asensio, "Intención," p. 91; Castro, *Hacia Cervantes,* p. 154;

Ricapito, "La cara de Dios," pp. 142–46; Sieber, *Language and Society,* pp. 19–21.

33. On the theme of cleanliness in this chapter and the next, see Donald McGrady, "Social Irony in *Lazarillo de Tormes* and its implications for Authorship," *Romance Philology* 23 (1970): 557–67.

34. Rico very perceptively points out the difference between what Lazarillo sees and what is reported to him, *La novela picaresca y el punto de vista,* pp. 38–39.

35. Some critics relate this to Jonah's three days in the belly of the whale. "Now the Lord prepared a great fish to swallow up Jonah. And Jonah was in the belly of the fish three days and three nights" (Jonah 1:17). "For as Jonah was three days and three nights in the whale's belly, so shall the Son of Man be there three days and three nights in the heart of the earth" (Matthew 12:40).

36. Tarr studies the hunger theme of the first three chapters, "Literary and Artistic Unity," pp. 406–12; Lázaro Carreter notes the significance of the number three in folklore and the novel, *Lazarillo en la picaresca,* pp. 91–97.

37. The author apparently knew Toledo and its environs very well. See Ricapito, *Lazarillo de Tormes,* p. 149; Asensio, "Intención," p. 96; Manuel Criado de Val, *Teoría de Castilla la Nueva: La dualidad castellana en los orígenes del español* (Madrid: Gredos, 1960), pp. 258–60.

38. A squire was the lowest rank of *hidalgos* ("nobles"), who barely eked out a living tending a knight's arms and serving him when there was no war. Lázaro Carreter studies the significance of the squire in folklore and literature, in *"Lazarillo" en la picaresca,* pp. 135–42.

39. After the third chapter, time accelerates until the culmination of Lázaro's "good fortune" in the last chapter. See Guillén, "La disposición temporal, del *Lazarillo de Tormes,*" *Hispanic Review* 25 (1957). 264–79.

40. Throughout this chapter there are references to cleanliness. For a study of these references see Donald McGrady, "Social Irony," pp. 557–63; also Gilman, "Death of Lazarillo" p. 165, n. 67; Rico, *Lazarillo,* pp. lxiii–lxv.

41. Tarr, "Literary and Artistic Unity," p. 410.

42. Dámaso Alonso believes that this is the first and last time that a *pícaro* will feel such pity, "La novela española y su contribución a la novela realista moderna," *Cuadernos del idioma* (Buenos Aires) 1 (1965): 31.

43. Carey studies this conversation carefully, "Asides," pp. 129–30.

44. For a study on hypocrisy and role playing in the novel, see Everett W. Hesse, "The *Lazarillo* and the Playing of a Role," *Kentucky Romance Quarterly* 22 (1975): 61–76.

45. Castro sees in the ardent sense of aristocracy a possible contact with

Erasmian thought, *Aspectos del vivir hispánico* (Santiago, Chile: Cruz del Sur, 1949), pp. 45–46. Others take the author for a New Christian; see Ricapito, *Lazarillo de Tormes*, p. 164.

46. Claudio Guillén observes that this is the inscrutable God of the Old Testament and refers to Job 5:9 and Romans 11:33 (*Lazarillo de Tormes*, p. 158, n. 255). For me, this need not be the God of the Old Testament. God for Lazarillo is inscrutable be He of the Old or New Testament.

47. On this concept of honor, see Fernando Lázaro Carreter, "Construcción y sentido del *Lazarillo de Tormes*," *Ábaco* 1 (1969): 133; Blecua, *Lazarillo de Tormes*, p. 137, n. 212; McGrady, "Social Irony," p. 565; Gilman, "Death of Lazarillo," pp. 150–52. For a possible connection with Erasmus's ideas on honor, see Ricapito, *Lazarillo de Tormes*, p. 159, n. 55.

48. Don Quixote and Sancho Panza develop this type of relationship, especially in the second part of the novel. Huck Finn and Jim and, more recently, Joe Buck and Ratso Rizzo in the film *Midnight Cowboy*, are outside the establishment and help one another to survive.

49. Notice that the narrator with his use of the word "today" brings his thoughts and observations up to the present time of narration. He implies that there are many like the Squire, even at the time he is writing the account of his life.

50. During this period in many parts of Europe the guilds were making economic advances and displacing people like the Squire. The upper classes became threatened by this advance, and in order to maintain their social position, they fantasized and created an ideal sense of honor. Some of the courtly literature of the time which idealized knights and their ladies probably was a reflection of their insecurity.

51. Bataillon sees a similarity here to the royal decree against beggars which was passed in 1540, and published in 1545, *Novedad y fecundidad del Lazarillo de Tormes*, trans. Luis Cortés Vázquez (Salamanca, 1968), p. 24.

52. For a study on the traditional aspects of this episode and its origins, see Francisco Ayala, *El "Lazarillo": nuevo examen de algunos aspectos* (Madrid, 1971), pp. 58–65, and Lázaro Carreter, *"Lazarillo" en la picaresca*, pp. 143–44. Deyermond, *Lazarillo*, p. 31, believes that given the persistent medieval attitudes in sixteenth-century Spain this episode emphasizes the dreadfulness of the grave and may not be out of character at all.

53. Martín de Riquer believes that the episode is out of place here but that the author included it as a traditional joke because he wanted to emphasize the poverty in the house (*"La Celestina" y "Lazarillo"* [Barcelona: Vergara, 1959], p. 96).

54. Louis C. Pérez observes that Lazarillo never laughs outwardly, and his laughter, when it does occur, is suppressed. He laughs only to himself. "On Laughter in *Lazarillo de Tormes*," *Hispania* 43 (1969): 529–33.

55. Guillén, *Lazarillo*, p. 25. For observations on this part of the chapter, see A. Rumeau, "Notes au *Lazarillo* (*contóme su hacienda* et *de toda fuerza*)," *Les langues néolatines* 164 (1963): 1931; Joseph V. Ricapito, "Algunas observaciones más sobre contóme su hacienda," *Annali instituo universitario orientale* 15 (1973): 227–33.

56. For a study on the style and content of this chapter and its relationship to the rest of the novel, see Tarr, "Literary and Artistic Unity," pp. 412–15; Lázaro Carreter, *"Lazarillo de Tormes" en la picaresca,* pp. 157–59; Ayala, *El Lazarillo*, pp. 66–68; Raymond S. Willis, "Lazarillo and the Pardoner: The Artistic Necessity of the Fifth *Tractado,"* *Hispanic Review* 27 (1959): 267–79; Sicroff, "Sobre el estilo," pp. 165–76; and Sieber, *Language and Society*, pp. 45–58.

57. Some critics have noted the difference between the epigraphs and the material that follows them and have concluded that the epigraphs were added at a later time. Tarr thinks that they were hastily written and mechanically inserted, p. 415.

58. Bataillon, *Novedad,* p. 20.

59. See Blecua, *Lazarillo*, p. 157, n. 287.

60. See Fred Abrams, "A Note on the Mercedarian Friar in the *Lazarillo de Tormes,"* *Romance Notes* 11 (1969): 444–46.

61. Sieber, *Language and Society*, p. 51.

62. See Márquez Villanueva, "La actitud espiritual," p. 79; Molho, *Romans picaresques espagnols,* p. xxxix; Bataillon, *Novedad,* p. 72; Lázaro Carreter, *"Lazarillo" en la picaresca,* pp. 158–59; and Sieber, *Language and Society,* p. 58. Some critics have chosen to skip over this material or omit it altogether in their studies on the novel.

63. Tarr, "Literary and Artistic Unity," p. 413.

64. Willis maintains that the author's use of the third person disengages Lázaro from the sympathetic attendance of the reader ("Lazarillo," p. 275).

65. Ricapito, *"Lazarillo de Tormes* (chapter 5) and Masuccio's Fourth *Novella,"* *Romance Philology* 23, (1970): 305–11; see also Lázaro Carreter, *"Lazarillo" en la picaresca,* pp. 160–65.

66. Constables had the reputation of being unsavory characters.

67. It is here that the episode recalls Boccaccio's Brother Onion, *Decamaron*, VI, 10.

68. For a background on papal bulls and their role in Spanish society at this time see José Goñí Gaztambide, "Los cuestores en España y la regalia de indulgencias," *Hispania Sacra* 2 (1949): 26–43; Henry Charles Lea, *A History of Auricular Confessions and Indulgences in the Latin Church,* 3 vols. (Philadelphia: Lea Brothers & Co., 1896); Aristide Rumeau, "Notes au *Lazarillo:* 'despedir la bula,'" *Les langues néo-latines* 163 (1962): 2–7; for a good review of this subject, see Sieber, *Language and Society*, pp. 60–68.

69. Sieber, *Language and Society*, pp. 64–65.

70. Ibid., pp. 64–65, 67.

71. Lea states that Erasmus's description of sinners, who thought that buying bulls would eliminate their sins so that they could indulge in new ones, was correct, (*A History of Auricular Confessions*, p. 76).

72. Sieber, *Language and Society*, p. 80; Truman believes that Lázaro presents himself in a humorous way, "Parody and Irony," p. 604; C. B. Morris says that Lázaro feels like a different man and believes that it would not be dignified for him to be connected with the donkey any longer: "Lázaro and the Squire: 'Hombres de bien,' " *Bulletin of Hispanic Studies* 41 (1964): 238–41; George A. Shipley studies the shrewd calculation and rhetorical genius of the narrator: "A Case of Functional Obscurity: the Master Tambourine-Painter of *Lazarillo, Tratado VI,*" *Modern Language Notes* 97 (1982): 225–53.

73. These words are used in chapter 1 to describe Lázaro's father who: "confessed and did not deny and suffered persecution under justice."

74. Castro considered Lázaro's swearing on the host an irreverent act (*Hacia Cervantes*, p. 156).

75. "Insigne la ciudad en donde las mujeres eran mancebas de clérigos" ("illustrious is the city where women were mistresses of the clergy"), in Castro, *Hacia Cervantes*, p. 157. For a study on Lázaro's wife, see G. Álvarez, *Le thème de la femme dans la picaresque espagnol* (Groningen: Wolters, 1955); J. Cañedo, "Tres pícaras, el amor y la mujer," *Ibero-Romania* 1 (1969): 193–227.

76. For a study on hypocrisy, see Everett Hesse, "The *Lazarillo de Tormes* and the Playing of a Role," *Kentucky Romance Quarterly* 22 (1975): 61–76.

77. Ayala, *El Lazarillo*, pp. 80–81.

78. Ricapito, *Lazarillo*, pp. 15–24.

Chapter Six

1. Lázaro Carreter, *"Lazarillo de Tormes,"* pp. 20–22.

2. Castro, *Hacia Cervantes*, p. 137.

3. Bataillon, *Lazarillo*, p. 37. There is a Spanish translation of the introduction, *Novedad y fecundidad del "Lazarillo de Tormes,"* trans. Luis Cortés Vázquez (Salamanca, 1968).

4. Castro, *Hacia Cervantes*, p. 145; Bataillon, *Le roman picaresque: Introduction et notes* (Paris: Aubier, 1931), p. 3. Gilman, "Death of Lazarillo Tormes," p. 152.

5. Guillén, "La disposición temporal," pp. 264–79.

6. R. W. Truman in his "Lázaro de Tormes and the 'Homo Novus' Tradition," *Modern Language Review* 64 (1969): 62–67, notes that there was a great deal of contemporary literature about low-born persons who rise and achieve nobility and that this type of literature is burlesqued by

Lazarillo de Tormes. Truman observes in his *"Lazarillo de Tormes,* Petrarch's *De remediis adversae fortunae,* and Erasmus's *Praise of Folly,"* *Bulletin of Hispanic Studies* 52 (1975): 33–53, that the source of the tradition could be the *De remediis adversae fortunae* and that Erasmus's *Praise of Folly* may have stimulated the author to burlesque it. Ann Wiltrout had previously observed a similarity in content, criticism, and philosophy between the novel and Erasmus in *"*The *Lazarillo de Tormes* and Erasmus' *Opulentia sordida,"* *Romanische Forschungen* 81 (1979): 550–64.

7. Tarr, "Literary and Artistic Unity," pp. 404–21.

8. For a discussion of the work as a novel, see Lázaro Carreter, *"Lazarillo,"* pp. 61–68.

9. Howard Mancing, "The Deceptiveness of *Lazarillo de Tormes,"* *PMLA* 90 (1971): 426–31.

10. L. J. Woodward, "Author-Reader Relationship in the *Lazarillo del* [sic] *Tormes,"* *Forum for Modern Language Studies* 1 (1965): 43–53.

11. Deyermond, *Lazarillo,* p. 73. The asides, given in direct speech, help the reader to understand Lazarillo's reactions to events. See Carey, "Asides," pp. 119–34.

12. Deyermond, *Lazarillo,* pp. 57–60.

13. Blecua, *Lazarillo,* pp. 41–44.

14. Deyermond, *Lazarillo,* p. 57.

15. For an excellent study on the author's use of language see Víctor de la Concha, *Nueva lectura del "Lazarillo"* (Madrid, 1981), pp. 213–58.

16. Guillén, "La disposición temporal,"pp. 264–79; Margit Frenk Alatorre, "Tiempo y narrador en el *Lazarillo* (episodio del ciego)," *Nueva revista de filología hispánica* 24 (1975): 195–218.

17. For a study on time in narrative and the differences between *temps de l'histoire* and *temps de l'écriture,* see Oswald Ducrot and Tzvetan Todorov, *Dictionnaire encyclopédique des sciences du langage* (Paris: Seuil, 1972), pp. 398–404; see also Wayne C. Booth, *The Rhetoric of Fiction,* 10th ed. (Chicago: University of Chicago Press, 1973); and Gérard Genette, "Discours du récit: Essai de méthode," in *Figures III* (Paris: Seuil, 1972).

18. Percy Lubbock points out the differences of summary and scene in *The Craft of Fiction* (London: J. Cape, 1921); see also Norman Friedman, "Points of View of Fiction: The Development of a Critical Concept," *PMLA* 70 (1955): 1160–84.

19. The "worries of the King of France" could refer to the French defeat at Pavia and the captivity of Francis I (1525–26). Some critics have attempted to date the work by referring to this and other parts of the text.

20. The internal chronological time is studied by Guillén, "La disposición temporal," pp. 273–75.

21. Alatorre, *Tiempo y narrador,* p. 215.

22. For a study of the present and past and how and when they con-

verge, see Guillén, "La disposición temporal," p. 270; and Rico, *La novela picaresca*, p. 29.

Chapter Seven

1. George A. Shipley in his article, "The Critic as Witness for the Prosecution: Making the Case against Lázaro de Tormes," *PMLA* 97 (1982), studies the narrator's defense for his part in the "affair," and concludes that he presents a sanitized empathy-inducing Lazarillo in chapters 1–3 while he plays down the later years in Toledo, masking his role in the scandalous *ménage à trois*. Lázaro mounts a defense based on two fundamental persuasive strategies. The first, Shipley calls "expedient renaming" which he describes as "those sleights of pen by which Lázaro brazenly sells his sow's ear of life as a silk purse, calling his degradation prosperity, calling his fall a rise to the pinnacle, calling the record of his shame a testament worthy of wide publication and fame, calling his renegade thief of a father a fallen hero . . ." (p. 184). The device of expedient renaming is simple; the effects are not. The second strategy "recontextualization" is a more subtle device used by poets and defense attorneys. He describes a case in point. "Recontextualization: discovered with his fist in the bread basket, Lázaro would have us believe he is the baker. Recontextualization is what defendants are up to when they plead for 'putting this whole thing in proper context' " (p. 184). For Shipley the eccentric shape of the narrative is designed by its narrator to serve his needs. He swells the narration of his early years while masking the recent "Toledo Years." Beverly J. De Long-Tonelli believes that the brevity of the final chapters respond to the interiorization of a narrator who has realized that his personality can survive only by virtue of a compromise with reality ("La ambigüedad en el *Lazarillo de Tormes*," *Revista de estudios hispánicos* 10 [1977]: 378–89).

Selected Bibliography

PRIMARY SOURCES

1. Texts
Lazarillo de Tormes. Edited by Francisco Rico. Barcelona: Planeta, 1967.
A good text, introduction and notes which treat all of the basic prob-
lems and themes of the work.
Lazarillo de Tormes. Edited by Joseph V. Ricapito. Madrid: Cátedra,
1976. A well annotated edition with an excellent introduction.
Lazarillo de Tormes and El Abencerraje. Edited by Claudio Guillén. New
York: Dell, 1966. An excellent introduction and notes for the general
reader.
La novela picaresca española. Edited by Angel Valbuena Prat. 6th ed.
Madrid: Aguilar, 1968. The most extensive anthology available. Very
well edited.
La vida de Lazarillo de Tormes. Edited by José Caso González. Madrid:
Boletín de la Real Academia Española, 1967. The introduction
stresses the relationship of the three 1554 editions, but studies others
as well.
La vida de Lazarillo de Tormes. Edited by Royston O. Jones. Manchester:
Manchester University Press, 1963. A fine and useful edition with a
good introduction.
La vida de Lazarillo de Tormes y de sus fortunas y adversidades. Edited by
Adolfo Bonilla y San Martín. Madrid: Ruiz, 1915. Good introduction
which mentions a 1550 edition printed somewhere outside of Spain.
La vida de Lazarillo de Tormes y de sus fortunas y adversidades. Edited by
Julio Cejador y Frauca. Madrid: Espasa-Calpe, 1941. Introduction
deals basically with the book's authorship.
La vida de Lazarillo de Tormes y de sus fortunas y adversidades. Edited by
Everett Hesse and Harry F. Williams. Madison: University of Wiscon-
sin Press, 1948. A good edition which contains a short but important
essay by Américo Castro.
La vida de Lazarillo de Tormes y de sus fortunas y adversidades. Edited by
Alfredo Cavaliere. Naples: Giannini, 1955. The first modern scholar
to study in a scientific way the relationship of the three 1554 editions.
La vida de Lazarillo de Tormes y de sus fortunas y adversidades. Edited by

Alberto Blecua. Madrid: Castalia, 1974. A good critical edition with an excellent introduction and notes. The introduction treats textual problems in detail.

2. Translations

Fridericus Berghius' Partial Latin Translation of "Lazarillo de Tormes" and its Relationship to the Early "Lazarillo" Translations in Germany. Study and edition by Charlotte Lang Brancaforte. Madison: Hispanic Seminary of Medieval Studies, 1983.

Histoire de Gil Blas de Santillana par LeSage: Lazarillo de Tormes. Translated by Louis Viardot. Paris: Dubochet le Chevalier, 1846.

Lazzarino de Tormes. Translated by A. Gasparetti. Milan: Rizzoli, 1960.

Das Leben des Lazarillo von Tormes: Sein Glück und Unglück. Translated by R. Grossmann. Leipzig: Dieterich, 1949.

Leben und Wandel Lazaril von Tormes. Translated by Herman Tiemann. Hamburg: Maximilian, 1951.

The Life of Lazarillo de Tormes. His Fortunes and His Adversities. Translated by Harriet de Onís. Great Neck, N.Y.: Barron's, 1959.

The Life of Lazarillo de Tormes and his Fortunes and Adversities. Translated by Louis How. New York: Kennerly, 1917. Contains an important introduction and notes by Charles Philip Wagner.

The Life of Lazarillo de Tormes, his Fortunes and his Adversities. Translated by W. S. Merwin. New York: Doubleday, 1960.

The Pleasant Historie of Lazarillo de Tormes: Drawn out of Spanish by David Rowland of Angleseay. 1586. Reprint. Oxford: Blackwell, 1924.

Two Spanish Picaresque Novels: Lazarillo de Tormes and The Swindler [El Buscón]. Translated by Michael Alpert. Middlesex, England; Baltimore: Penguin, 1969.

La Vie de Lazarillo de Tormes. Translated by Albert Morel-Fatio. Paris: Aubier, 1958. Contains an introduction by Marcel Bataillon.

Vita e avventure de Lazzarino di Tormes. Translated by F. Carlesi. Lanciano: Carabba, 1917.

3. Bibliographies

Laurenti, Joseph. L. *Bibliografía de la literatura picaresca.* Metuchen, N.J.: Scarecrow Press, 1973. A good bibliography.

Ricapito, Joseph V. *Bibliografía razonada y anotada de las obras maestras de la novela picaresca española.* Madrid: Castalia, 1976. The most complete bibliography to date. Excellent summary of critical views on the novel and the major topics surrounding it. An essential book for the serious scholar.

SECONDARY SOURCES

Abrams, Fred. "A Note on the Mercedarian Friar in the *Lazarillo de Tormes.*" *Romance Notes* 11 (1969): 444–46. Studies the Monk with relation to satire.

———. "Hurtado de Mendoza's Concealed Signatures in the *Lazarillo de Tormes.*" *Romance Notes* 15 (1973): 341–45. Cryptographic analysis of "Pues sepa Vuestra Merced ante todas cosas. . . ."

Alfaro, Gustavo A. *La estructura de la novela picaresca.* Bogotá: Instituto Caro y Cuervo, 1977. Classifies three types of *pícaros:* true *pícaros,* student *pícaros,* and *anti-pícaros.*

Alter, Robert. *Rogue's Progress: Studies in the Picaresque Novel.* Cambridge: Harvard University Press, 1964. Chapter 1 treats the picaresque and *Lazarillo de Tormes.* Later writers such as Lesage, Defoe, and Smollett are also studied.

Asensio, Manuel J. "La intención religiosa del *Lazarillo de Tormes* y Juan de Valdés," *Hispanic Review* 26 (1959): 78–102. An important analysis of the religious attitudes of Toledo and its surroundings in 1525.

Ayala, Francisco. *El Lazarillo: nuevo examen de algunos aspectos.* Madrid: Taurus, 1971. Brief study with some interesting insights.

Bataillon, Marcel. *El sentido del Lazarillo de Tormes.* Paris: Librairie des Editions Espagnoles, 1954. A study on sources.

———. *Novedad y fecundidad del Lazarillo de Tormes.* 2d ed. Salamanca: Anaya, 1973. Translation of the introduction to his 1958 edition of *Lazarillo de Tormes.* An indispensable study.

Bell, A. "The Rhetoric of Self-Defense of Lázaro de Tormes." *Modern Language Review* 68 (1973): 84–93. Good insights into the relationship between the fictional pseudoautobiographer and his text.

Bjornson, Richard. *The Picaresque Hero in European Fiction.* Madison: University of Wisconsin Press, 1977. An excellent general study on the picaresque. Well documented and written.

Blackburn, Alexander. *The Myth of the Pícaro: Continuity and Transformation of the Picaresque Novel 1554–1954.* Chapel Hill: University of North Carolina Press, 1979.

Blanco Aguinaga, Carlos. "Cervantes y la picaresca: Notas sobre dos tipos de realismo." *Nueva revista de filología hispánica* 11 (1957), 314–42. English translation: "Cervantes and the Picaresque Mode: Notes on Two Kinds of Realism," in *Cervantes: A Collection of Critical Essays, Twentieth Century Views,* edited by Lowry J. Nelson, Englewood Cliffs, N.J.: Prentice Hall, 1969, pp. 137–51 (abridged). Contrasts Cervantes's narrative technique with that of the picaresque.

Blanquat, Josett. "Fraude et frustration dans *Lazarillo de Tormes.*" In *Culture et marginalités au 16ème siècle,* by José L. Alonso Hernández et al. Paris: Klincksieck, 1973, pp. 41–73.

Brancaforte, Benito, and Brancaforte, Charlotte, eds. *La primera traducción del 'Lazarillo de Tormes' por Giulio Strozzi.* Ravenna: A. Longo, 1977. This is the rendering of the Antwerp edition of 1554 together with the anonymous second part of 1555.

Carey, Douglas M. "Asides and Interiority in *Lazarillo de Tormes:* A Study in Psychological Realism." *Studies in Philology* 66 (1969): 119–34. An imaginative and well documented study.

Castro, Américo. *Hacia Cervantes.* Madrid: Taurus, 1957. Contains insightful material on *Lazarillo de Tormes.*

Chandler, Frank Wadleigh. *Romances of Roguery.* 1899. Reprint. New York: Burt Franklin, 1961. A pioneer study which is still readable. Valuable bibliography and information on early editions and translations.

Concha, Víctor G. de la. "La intención religiosa del *Lazarillo.*" *Revista de filología española* 55 (1972): 243–77. Religious material well documented and discussed.

———. *Nueva lectura del "Lazarillo."* Madrid: Castalia, 1981. A very useful study which includes insightful material on structure, language, and themes of the novel.

De Haan, Fonger. *An Outline of the "Novela Picaresca" in Spain.* The Hague: Nijhoff, 1903. Brief and readable.

Del Monte, Alberto. *Itinerario de la novela picaresca.* Barcelona: Lumen, 1971. Translation of the Italian original, *Itinerario del romanzo picaresco spagnolo* (Firenze: Sansoni, 1957). An excellent study with numerous well written notes.

De Long-Tonelli, Beverly J. "La ambigüedad narrativa en el *Lazarillo de Tormes.*" *Revista de estudios hispánicos,* 10 (1977): 378–89. Includes a good explanation of the brevity and acceleration of the final three chapters.

Deyermond, Alan D. *"Lazarillo de Tormes": A Critical Guide.* London: Grant and Cutler, 1975. An excellent study for the general reader and the professional as well.

Dunn, Peter N. *The Spanish Picaresque Novel.* Boston: Twayne Publishers, 1979. A useful and well documented study for the general reader.

Durand, Frank. "The Author and Lázaro: Levels of Comic Meaning." *Bulletin of Hispanic Studies* 45 (1968): 89–101. A careful analysis of the humor in the work and its relationship to theme.

Fiore, Robert. *"Lazarillo de Tormes:* estructura narrativa de una novela picaresca." In *La picaresca: Orígenes, textos y estructuras,* edited by

Manuel Criado del Val. Madrid: Fundacion Universitaria Española, 1979, pp. 359–66.

———. *"Lazarillo de Tormes* and *Midnight Cowboy:* The Picaresque Model and Myth."* In *Studies in Honor of Everett W. Hesse,* edited by William C. McCrary and José A. Madrigal. Lincoln: Society of Spanish and Spanish-American Studies, 1981, pp. 81–97.

Francis, Alan. *Picaresca, decadencia, historia: Aproximación a una realidad histórico-literaria.* Madrid: Gredos, 1978. Examines the three dominant themes of honor, religion, and the vision of Spain.

Frenk Alatorre, Margit. "Tiempo y narrador en el *Lazarillo* (Episodio del ciego)." *Nueva revista de filología hispánica* 24 (1975): 197–218. An excellent study on time.

Frohock, W. M. "The Failing Center: Recent Fiction and the Picaresque Tradition." *Novel* 3 (1969): 62–69. Mentions the misuse of the term picaresque.

———. "The Idea of the Picaresque." *Yearbook of Comparative and General Literature* 16 (1967): 43–52. Raises the issue of the responsible use of the term picaresque.

Gilman, Stephen. "The Death of Lazarillo de Tormes." *PMLA* 81 (1966): 149–66. A study noted for its perceptive observations on structure, style, and theme. Well written and documented.

Guillén, Claudio. "La disposición temporal del *Lazarillo de Tormes.*" *Hispanic Review* 25 (1957): 264–79. A study with some brilliant insights. It has affected a great deal of later criticism.

———. *Literature as System.* Princeton: Princeton University Press, 1971. Includes excellent essays on the picaresque that are clearly written, well documented, and perceptive.

Herrero, Javier. "The Great Icons of the *Lazarillo:* The Bull, The Wine, The Sausage and The Turnip." *Ideologies and Literature* 1 (1978): 3–18. An insightful study.

———. "Renaissance Poverty and Lazarillo's Family: The Birth of the Picaresque Genre." *PMLA* 94 (1979): 876–86. Studies in detail poverty as a social issue reflected in the work.

Hesse, Everett W. "The *Lazarillo de Tormes* and the Playing of a Role." *Kentucky Romance Quarterly* 22 (1975): 61–76. An insightful study on hypocrisy.

———. "The *Lazarillo de Tormes* and the Way of the World." *Revista de estudios hispánicos.* 11 (1977): 163–80. Analyzes the degradation in the novel and how Lázaro has accepted it.

Jones, C.A. "*Lazarillo de Tormes:* Survival or Precursor?" In *Litterae hispanae et lusitanae,* edited by Hans Flasche. Munich: Hueber, 1968, pp. 181–88. Considers the medieval tradition of the work.

Jones, R. O. *A Literary History of Spain.* New York: Barnes and

Noble, 1971. A good study for the general reader and the scholar.

Lázaro Carreter, Fernando. "Construcción y sentido de *'Lazarillo de Tormes.'*" *Ábaco* 1 (1969): 45-134. Good study on structure and themes, much of which appears in *"Lazarillo" en la picaresca*.

———. *"Lazarillo de Tormes" en la picaresca*. Barcelona: Ariel, 1972. A seminal study with some excellent insights on structure, style, and themes.

Lida de Malkiel, María Rosa. "Función del cuento popular en el *Lazarillo de Tormes*." In *Actas del I Congreso Internacional de Hispanistas*. Oxford: Dolphin, 1964, pp. 349-59. The first good study on folklore and its relation to the novel's structure.

Lomax, Derek W. "On Re-Reading the *Lazarillo de Tormes*." In *Studia Iberica: Festschrift für Hans Flasche*. Bern: Francke, 1973, pp. 349-59. Treats poverty and clerical immorality in an insightful way.

McGrady, Donald. "Social Irony in *Lazarillo de Tormes* and its Implications for Authorship." *Romance Philology* 23 (1970): 557-67. Studies the *converso* problem.

Madrigal, José A. "El simbolismo como vehículo temático en el *Lazarillo de Tormes*." In *La picaresca: Orígenes, textos, y estructuras*, edited by Manuel Criado de Val. Madrid: Fundación Universitaria Española, 1979, pp. 405-12. An insightful study on symbolism.

Mancing, Howard. "The Deceptiveness of *Lazarillo de Tormes*." *PMLA* 90 (1975): 426-32. A good study that points out the relationship between Lazarillo and Lázaro and how it affects readers.

———. "The Picaresque Novel: A Protean Form." *College Literature* 6 (1979): 182-204. A general introduction to the picaresque.

Márquez Villanueva, F. "La actitud espiritual del *Lazarillo de Tormes*." In *Espiritualidad y literatura en el siglo xvi* pp. 30-38; 67-137. Madrid: Alfaguara, 1968. Good study on religious and philosophical views of the author.

Miller, Stuart. *The Picaresque Novel*. Cleveland: Case Western Reserve University Press, 1967. Treats an ideal genre type.

Molho, Maurice. *Romans picaresques espagnols*. Paris: Gallimard, 1978. A good introduction which was translated as *Introducción al pensamiento picaresco* (Salamanca: Anaya, 1972).

Morreale, Margherita. "Reflejos de la vida española en el *Lazarillo*." *Clavileño*, no. 30 (1954), pp. 28-31. Studies interesting documents of the *Cortes* (Parliament).

Morris, C.B. "Lázaro and the Squire: *Hombres de bien*." *Bulletin of Hispanic Studies* 41 (1964): 238-41. Demonstrates how Lázaro follows the Squire's example and adopts his doctrines.

Nepaulsingh, Colbert I. "Lázaro's Fortune." *Romance Notes* 20 (1980): 417-23. A study on fortune, virtue, and vice.

Parr, James A. "La estructura satírica del *Lazarillo*." In *La picaresca:*

Orígenes, textos y estructuras, edited by Manuel Criado de Val. Madrid: Fundación Universitaria Española, 1979, pp. 376–84. Interesting study which relates *Lazarillo de Tormes* to the form of the Novel.

Perry, T. Anthony. "Biblical Symbolism in the *Lazarillo de Tormes.*" *Studies in Philology* 67 (1970): 139–46. Interesting insights.

Piper, Anson C. "The Breadly Paradise of *Lazarillo de Tormes.*" *Hispania* 44 (1961): 269–71. A valuable study on the symbolic significance of the battle of the chest in chapter 2.

Ricapito, Joseph V. "Algunas observaciones más sobre 'contóme su hacienda.'" *Annali Istituto Universitario Orientale* 15 (1973): 227–33. Treats the episode of the squire.

———. "Cara de Dios: Ensayo de rectificación." *Bulletin of Hispanic Studies* 50 (1973): 142–46. A well reasoned study of the religious and moral aspects of the phrase "cara de Dios" ("face of God").

———. "*Lazarillo de Tormes* (chap. 5) and Masuccio's Fourth *Novella.*" *Romance Philology* 23 (1970): 305–11. Studies a possible source of the chapter on the pardoner.

———. "Two Facets of Renaissance Perspective: *Lazarillo de Tormes* and Machiavelli." *Romanische Forschungen* 82 (1971): 151–72. Compares *Mandragola* to the novel.

Rico, Francisco. "En torno al texto crítico del *Lazarillo de Tormes.*" *Hispanic Review* 38 (1970): 405–19.

———. *La novela picaresca y el punto de vista.* Barcelona: Seix Barral, 1970. Second edition of this excellent work was printed in 1973. Valuable insights.

———. "Problemas del *Lazarillo.*" *Boletín de la Real Academia Española* 96 (1966): 277–96. Studies the *caso* and how it governs thematic aspects of the work.

Ruffinato, A. *Struttura e significazione del "Lazarillo de Tormes."* 2 vols. Turin: Giappichelli, 1977. A thorough study on structure and style.

Scordilis Brownlee, Marina. "Expansion and Generic Subversion: The Two Continuations of *Lazarillo de Tormes.*" *Philological Quarterly* 61 (1982): 317–25. A good study of the anonymous *Segunda parte de Lazarillo de Tormes* and that of Juan de Luna.

Shipley, George A. "A Case of Functional Obscurity: The Master Tambourine-Painter of *Lazarillo, Tratado VI.*" *Modern Language Notes* (1982): 225–53. Insightful study on the rhetorical genius of the narrator.

———. "The Critic as Witness for the Prosecution: Making the Case against Lázaro de Tormes." *PMLA* 97 (1982): pp. 179–94. A good study on the narrator's defense and the structure of the novel.

———. "The Critic as Witness for the Prosecution: Resting the Case Against Lázaro de Tormes." In *Creation and Re-Creation: Ex-*

periments in Literary Form in Early Modern Spain. Newark, Del.: Juan de la Cuesta, 1983. Good study on irony and narrative technique.

Sicroff, Albert A. "Sobre el estilo del *Lazarillo de Tormes.*" *Nueva revista de filología hispánica* 11 (1957): 157–70. Contains some valuable insights.

Siebenmann, Gustav. *Ueber Sprache und stil im Lazarillo de Tormes.* Bern: Franke, 1953. The first three chapters contain a good study on language, the final chapters relate language to style.

Sieber, Harry. *Language and Society in "Lazarillo de Tormes."* Baltimore: Johns Hopkins University Press, 1978. A provocative study on language, structure, and style. Some good insights.

———. *The Picaresque.* London: Methuen, 1977. Brief but useful general study.

Suárez-Galbán, Eugenio. "Caracterización literaria e ideología social en el *Lazarillo de Tormes.*" In *La picaresca: Orígenes, textos y estructuras,* edited by Manuel Criado de Val. Madrid: Fundación Universitaria Española, 1979, pp. 469–77. A well documented study on style and Lázaro's social class.

Tarr, F. Courtney. "Literary and Artistic Unity in the *Lazarillo de Tormes.*" *PMLA* 42 (1927): 404–21. The foundation of modern criticism on *Lazarillo de Tormes,* veritably a pioneer study in the field.

Truman, R. W. "Lázaro de Tormes and the *Homo novus* tradition." *Modern Language Review* 64 (1969): 62–67. Studies the virtuous self-made man.

———. "*Lazarillo de Tormes,* Petrarch's *De remediis adversae fortunae,* and Erasmus's *Praise of Folly.*" *Bulletin of Hispanic Studies* 52 (1975): 33–53. A good comparative study on themes.

———. "Parody and Irony in the Self-Portrayal of Lázaro de Tormes." *Modern Language Review* 63 (1968): 600–605. Studies the use of parody and humor. Valuable insights.

Vranich, S. B. "El caso del Lazarillo: un estudio semántico en apoyo de la unidad estructural de la novela." In *La picaresca: Orígenes, textos y estructuras,* edited by Manuel Criado de Val. Madrid: Fundación Universitaria Española, 1979, pp. 367–74. An insightful study on language in the novel.

Wardropper, Bruce W. "El trastorno de la moral en el *Lazarillo.*" *Nueva revista de filología hispánica* 15 (1961): 441–47. An excellent study on the significance of the word *bueno* ("good") in the novel.

———. "The Implications of Hypocrisy in the *Lazarillo de Tormes.*" In *Studies in Honor of Everett W. Hesse,* edited by William C. McCrary and José Madrigal. Lincoln: Society of Spanish and Spanish-American Studies, 1981, pp. 179–86. Shows how hypocrisy pervades the novel.

————. "The Strange Case of Lázaro González Pérez." *Modern Language Notes* 92 (1977): 202–12.

Weiner, Jack. *El ciego y las dos hambres de Lázaro de Tormes.* Serie de monografías. Universidad Católica de Valparaíso, Chile. Valparaíso: Instituto de Lenguas y Literaturas, 1971, pp. 1–36. A thorough and well-documented study.

————. "La lucha de Lazarillo de Tormes por el arca." In *Actas del Tercer Congreso Internacional de Hispanistas,* edited by Carlos H. Magis. Mexico City: Colegio de Mexico, 1969, pp. 931–34. Interprets the battle in religious and allegorical terms.

Whitbourne, Christine J. "Moral Ambiguity in the Spanish Picaresque Tradition." In *Knaves and Swindlers: Essays on the Picaresque Novel in Europe.* London: Oxford University Press, 1974, pp. 1–24. Good for the general reader.

Wicks, Ulrich. "The Nature of Picaresque Narrative: A Modal Approach." *PMLA* 89 (1974): 240–49. An extremely helpful study which shows a way of avoiding problems with the extreme definitions of the picaresque.

————. "*Pícaro,* Picaresque: The Picaresque in Literary Scholarship." *Genre* 5 (1972): 153–92. Studies the issue of whether picaresque fiction is an historical phenomenon or a universal form.

Willis, Raymond S. "Lazarillo and the Pardoner: The Artistic Necessity of the Fifth *Tractado.*" *Hispanic Review* 27 (1959): 267–79. An excellent study on the abrupt structural change in the novel.

Wiltrout, Ann. "The *Lazarillo de Tormes* and Erasmus' *Opulentia Sordida.*" *Romanische Forschungen* 81 (1969): 550–64. Studies the similarity of style, criticism, and philosophy in the two works.

Woods, M. J. "Pitfalls for the Moralizer in *Lazarillo de Tormes.*" *Modern Language Review* 74 (1979): 590–98. Warns of self-deception and misreading the text.

Woodward, L. J. "Author-Reader Relationship in the *Lazarillo del* [sic] *Tormes.*" *Forum for Modern Language Studies* 1 (1965): 45–53. Good study on narrative structure and character development.

Ziomeck, H. "El *Lazarillo de Tormes* y *La vida inútil de Pito Pérez:* Dos novelas picarescas." In *Actas del Tercer Congreso Internacional de Hispanistas,* edited by Carlos H. Magis. Mexico City: Colegio de Mexico, 1969, pp. 945–54. Good comparative study.

Index